1985

Collected Poems

Collected Poems
E. L. MAYO

Edited and with an Introduction by David Ray

A *New Letters* Book
University of Missouri - Kansas City

SWALLOW PRESS
OHIO UNIVERSITY PRESS
Chicago   Athens, Ohio   London

ISBN 0-938652-00-1
Library of Congress Catalog No. 80-84519

Swallow Press Books
(including New Letters Books)
are published by
Ohio University Press
Athens, Ohio 45701

Collected Poems by E. L. Mayo is a Memorial Edition:
we gratefully acknowledge the help of the
Drake University Centennial Committee.

Grateful acknowledgement is hereby tendered to the editors of
magazines that, in addition to *New Letters*, published E. L.
Mayo's work during his lifetime: *American Prefaces, Contact,
Contemporary Poetry, Epoch, Iowa English Yearbook, The
Nation, New Statesman, New York Times, North American
Mentor, Northwest Review, Platform, Poetry, Poetry Northwest,
Truth, T.L.S., University of Kansas City Review.* We are also grate-
ful to Twayne & to the U. of Minnesota Press, who brought out his
three individual titles, repeated as sections here. We are particularly
admiring of Carroll Coleman who hand set the 1973 *Selected
Poems* for his Prairie Press in Iowa City; that edition shows the
love and aesthetic craft of the American small press scene at its best.

FIRST EDITION

CONTENTS

From Manuscript

For Myra

It was as much your project as mine, darling,
To make these poems out of experience.
The mighty shadow of a god still hung
Over the countryside when we began;
Now it is dissipated, a wisp here
And there, elsewhere mere sky,
Sunset apart, darkens toward evening.
But why should I, why should you, care?
Shall we not take night in good countenance?
Now in their hordes and herds the stars appear.
Come, let us watch, before we join the dance.

From a Journal dated 1961 on the flyleaf

The true poem fuses the actual with the ideal, or, more truly,
renders the fact transparent so that human feeling and the ideal
come through it like light through a diamond. This prism is
the *unity* a poem can frame which the average modern individual
lacks. For in our lives we are scattered, dissociated. A good poem
about anything reminds us of our lost unity and impels us to
seek it.

—E. L. MAYO

Preface

In 1947 a classically-trained, cragged-faced poet from the North came to Drake and for 25 years the magic of his voice and eye, the insights of his poetry, the loving concern he showed for his students and for poets everywhere graced our campus. To those of us who shared his corner of the campus he gave a little more capacity to live with life's dilemmas and to recognize life's incongruities. He was a selfless spirit, an unmoved mover who annually drew poets from all over the state—at their own expense—to read and talk the night away. As he cherished the values of cooperation and understanding, he neatly undermined hypocrisy and rhodomontade; his poetry was self-analytical in the best sense, neither prideful nor confessional, and nothing human was alien to him.

Among his students who turned out to be productive in later years are Robert Dana, Ben Howard, Ira Levin, Robert Hullihan, Lauro Martines, Mary Mayo, Donn Brannon, Lee Hadley, and Sandra Greifenstein. But there is no way of reckoning how many of his students came to share a little of his love of poetry and his receptiveness to all aspects of life.

—TED STROUD
The Drake University Centennial Committee
Des Moines, Iowa

E. L. Mayo, 1972   *Bob Barrett*

Introduction

E. L. Mayo was, for a few of us, something of a father figure. He was a bit of the quiet shaman, witty and curative in his views, gentle and forgiving, sharp with insight but amused and non-acerbic. When we had the opportunity to talk with him, we experienced the satisfying of a deep and too-often denied hunger. He offered us the views of a man who had achieved a disinterested and amused tolerance for the world and its disappointments, its sorrows, but also its small triumphs. No one who met him could doubt that he sought wisdom, and had found some of its comforts, and that he knew also of its denials. He asked very little for himself, but certainly he insisted on those basic necessities, his books and journals and pens and the time to do what he really loved to do, which was to think and to create poems. He embraced obscurity almost as a condition for his intellectual freedom; in turn that freedom was an essential condition for the creation of these poems.

Still, a few discerning critics noticed Ed Mayo's quiet achievement. In 1958, James Wright wrote in *Poetry* that the Mayo poems "smolder with a kind of subdued bitterness," and he praised the work as "unpretentious." He found the poet "daring and successful precisely because he does not overburden his language." The *Summer Unbound* volume, he said, was "severe, tough," with a natural modernity.

John Ciardi has praised Mayo's "intellectual fire," "verbal felicity," and capacity to create symbols and images that conspire toward a "sudden burgeoning of second meanings." He saw in this work "happy evidence of how far poetry has come in a hundred years toward acquiring a wholly natural mastery of the commonest details of ordinary living." Ciardi put some of Mayo's work, along with an interview, in his influential anthology, *Mid-Century American Poets*, and certainly from that time Ed Mayo became for many of us "a poet's poet," not widely appreciated by the general public, but certainly an admired craftsman, practitioner of the art of poetry at its best. All too often in today's poetry there is nothing but surface meaning. Mayo's readers, like Eliot's or Stevens's, had to go beneath those surfaces, had to take a dive. Perhaps that's why Ed Mayo named a poem and then an entire book, *The Diver*. He was probably familiar with Neruda's "Ode to the Diver":

> Like all the things
> that I learned
> in my existence,
> studying them, knowing them,
> did I learn that to be a diver
> is a difficult
> profession? No!
> Infinite.

The wisdom of compromise and acceptance, adjustment and yielding, was expressed in Mayo's "Iron Gate."

> Here Solomon perceives he is not wise
> And with an eye upon the second prize
> Divides desire with possibility . . .
> The sea gull in his proper breast
> Beats louder now against a thinner door . . .

These lines do not, of course, share the much-lauded wisdom of the suicide poets who, like Medea, eloquently announce that "Life has been cruel to me" and then rush from one corner of the stage to the other raging and murdering most glamorously, till we forget that even self-murder is still "murder most foul" and a hell of an example to the young, who after all watch us more closely than the weather. Clearly Mayo realized, somewhere around mid-life, that he would not have, could not have, what Myra Mayo describes as: "not *acclaim*, but the knowledge that his voice was heard—perhaps enough response to it to reassure him on this point. He knew he was saying something important, but the feeling that he was saying it to nobody—a vacuum—could be overwhelming." But that failure, if it could be foolishly labeled such, drove him on and opened up new wells of creativity. He said it in a poem, thanking those powers that had denied his pettier, more selfish, quest. It is a three line poem entitled "Failure":

> Failure is more important than success
> Because it brings intelligence to light
> The bony structure of the universe.

"Even the awkward song is excellent," the poet wrote, and "from the bland, snow-crusted eminence / of sixty" he compared himself to "a mild smiling Cheshire gentleman / cat of sixty fading softly away." But like Williams in "The Descent" he praised the process: "My vision will continue to expand / Brobdingnagian / Until I comprehend all humankind / Without being there."

Robert Hullihan, in a *Des Moines Register* profile in the year of Ed's death, described the poet as something of a spy, a man with a secret vision and a penchant for codes:

> When he was younger and deeply involved in espionage the authorities took little notice of him, even though he was one of the leading agents for a government unknown to this day.
>
> He walked about with a kind of ill-fitted vigor that made him seem harmless. He was skilled in seeming to approach some casual destination that would suddenly divide and become two destinations at once, or several.
>
> And so he was never captured even though he did not employ a cipher and always wrote his reports in clear language.
>
> That was dangerous but necessary for his mission was, as he recalls it now in retirement "to make things mean more than they mean; to compose a structure that common sense tells you just isn't there at all."
>
> It was hazardous, profitless work in a country intent upon making things mean less than they mean.
>
> But Edward Mayo persisted all through the 27 years when he seemed to be a professor of English at Drake University in Des Moines.
>
> Of course, there was always some suspicion that he was something more than that . . . .

Edward Mayo is a poet who only called himself a spy once by way of explaining where the poet is and what he does:

"Someone who watches and writes things down and sends in reports from the midst of the human uproar. A spy, if you like."

"Yes, I remember. And I still believe that," said Mayo, nodding into the smoke like a patriarch tending to a sacrificial fire. He has a face molded for stern judgment except that it is incapable of rebuke.

"A spy, trying to see through the apparent to the something behind it that is something more," he said.

Mayo was a Metaphysical, and his poems gain in power because of the tension between the metaphysical, the occasionally obscure or at least demanding references, and the idiomatic. The poems "pretend to be simple prose-like utterances," David Daiches noted, "whereas in fact the best of them contain an echoing poetic meaning which begins to release itself a split second after we have read the words. There is an assumed lightness of touch here, a note not quite of irony but almost of timidity, behind which the richer meanings can be heard. . . . . He understands what form does to an idea, and is not afraid to write something which is in itself trivial but in its poetic context is not." Other critics tried to define that elusive and unique quality not often found among "the clichés which make much modern poetry seem a kaleidoscope in which the same unevocative images and abstractions are constantly reshuffled into new patterns." Mayo followed up mysteries, sought "the true, secret name of the river," opened up "the mystery of better and of worse," negotiated with that angel whose "name was Loneliness." And he knew that flesh is only a door, behind which we hear the "Wind—I said—Breaker of ties, breaker of promises." The human is always betrayed, and yet "The jungles of the sea must flower still." Poetry, he said, was a "mirror, showing / Clearer than to our shadowy sense, the glowing / And waning of a more than mortal creature." Just as "moles are very little / And worlds are very big," so the poet and his world must work and live together, unfairly matched. Out of such tension an occasional miracle emerges, hence Mayo's "El Greco" sonnet.

Such poems must not be lost to future generations. It may seem extravagant to say so, but E. L. Mayo devoted his life to the purity of thought, and he generously passes on to us findings of great value. If we're into throwing away clear messages from the stars received on our most subtle astronomical telescopes, precisely beamed, then we should indeed disregard and tear up his poems, or let them gather in out-of-the-way magazines and anthologies. But that queue of the generations coming will need all he has left them, and we must pray they will not forget how to read, not at all an unlikely possibility.

Ed Mayo was not, then, an idle collector of images, a man who sets his typewriter down on his crate and looks around the room for something to list. Nor was he a seeker of fashions; he didn't even live in the right place. And he had not the slightest idea of how to promote his own work. (I suspect that was itself one of his ideas.) Modesty made him rare. At last indifferent to acclaim he might have sought, he pursued his own light as devotedly as had Emerson; he gave everything he had to his writing, and because he was a learned man, that writing was an activity almost inseparable from his teaching. Not only did he teach for many years at Drake University, he is still teaching, through his poems.

Some of Mayo's poems of close family feeling, his elegy for his father and his "Letter to My Grandfather's Picture," are as vivid as Lewis W. Hine's photographs capturing the music of farm and mill. Mayo respects the crucial, inspiring link between generations, and he asks the ultimate question of our mission on earth:

> We never see the thing we have worked on
> Whirling from revolution to revolution
> Through the Mill's long explosion.
> Yet do not lean out of the picture, Grandfather;
> Though you cried out like Jesus and Jehovah
> I could not hear you through the spindles' roar.

A heavier worry runs through "A Reassurance," with its "Preoccupation / With liquefaction falling on our world," the atomic nightmare that threatens to undo all philosophy:

> You can't unthink, you can't unlink again
> The Hiroshima chain. Our marriage rite
> Was the bridal of the earth and sky.

A persistent image for Mayo is that of the perilous perch, the endangered grip. "Nature is innocent / Of nothing, nothing." He compared our lives to those of pioneer children, ever vulnerable. And yet the only solution is an affirmation of will:

> As pioneering children, when no rain
> Made water brackish in the last canteen,
> Went right to sleep, and just as seldom knew
> When guns were cocked and ready all night through,
> So do we ride the earth's revolving wheel,
> Moving across what prairies, to what wars,
> Against what ambush, eye does not reveal;
> Nor do we know what loyal outriders
> Swing on to clear our path across the plain,
> But drift to sleep where canvas hides the stars
> Of the long planetary wagon train.
>
> ("Wagon Train")

Mayo was always a Platonist, knew that the eternal forms were real, though threatened by "variably-defined Necessity." Beauty and Love were the most threatened, and poetry aspires not only to know them but to protect and perpetuate them. Nature provides merely occasions for discovering truths:

> We neither knew
> A trumpet blew nor felt the whole world shake;
> Yet children playing with the evidence
> That soul is form and does the body make
> Wake us with their shrill cries: the news is true:
> The forms of things endure and glister through.
>
> ("Ice Storm")

E. L. Mayo has many such truths for us.

—DAVID RAY
University of Missouri-Kansas City

The Diver

The Diver

Dressed in his clumsy, stiff, aquatic clothes,
His helmet screwed fast on so that he can
Do, say, see nothing in the world of man,
The diver shambles to the boatside, goes
Down the ladder, and the waters close
Over the steel that seals his sacred brain.
Over the boatside lean, his shadow scan
As it descends, shapeless and wavering.
It is no devilfish, is still a man—
But now it's gone.
                  Creatures beyond our ken
He will describe in words on his return—
Pale words for objects seen—
The inhuman life that swirled before his sight,
Or fled, or fought. The treasure he seeks out
May yet be lifted up by creaking crane,
Splashing, out of the green, but in his brain
The jungles of the sea must flower still,
Whose hook has drawn the pale blood of the shark,
And when his streaming bulk climbs back aboard,
We'll mutter, say some contract has been signed
With what lies under, and that that occurred
Which has no human gesture and no word.

The Dance of the Feather

You have seen me do the dance of the dagger;
Next I shall perform the dance of the feather;
This is more difficult, yet easier, too.
In the first the blades are not supposed to touch you
But sometimes do; in the second you float around
As though held up by something invisible,
And sometimes the breeze lets you down,
But that is a part of the dance, an integral part:
Feathers don't fall like iron, of course,
But gradually, until everybody sees
It's drifting down at forty-five degrees
Or thereabouts, an inch above the floor,
And then some warm wind coming under a door
Finds the gray fluff and sends it up again—
Not far, not long—you never can be sure
Where it is going, what it's going to do—
That too is a part of the dance and half its charm.
Eventually of course it comes down,
Or at least I think it does—that isn't clear,
And sometimes halfway through I get a new idea.

A Poem Is a Mirror

A poem is a mirror held to nature,
But it should be a magic mirror, showing
Clearer than to our shadowy sense, the glowing
And waning of a more than mortal creature,

And like calm stars above the anxious wind
Poems should allay with presentness our aching
For phantoms and their fashion of forsaking—
More tangible than earth, more real than mind.

The Long Way

You always know, and knew
You have forever not to speak a word—
The groves there, stirred
By no hail, no wind.

You always choose, therefore,
The other, the long way—
The rocky ledge by the sea,
Hairy with sea-grass, glare
Sun without shadow. This

Is the best and the worst.
It does not last long:
The beach at once gives way
To the Concessions,

(The children, amphibians, expend
On water and on shore a summer's day,
But tanneries and mills where hides are cut
Is where their years are put),

Behind the canvas mountains, tenements:
Here, if you have a cent,
After pop, popcorn, lemonade,
You take the ferry, blunt at either end,
The common, general expedient.

Then the train takes your sunburned nausea
(A good day never dies)
With heat, with cinders, and with memories.

And subways squeal and turning turnstiles say
"Come, come away,
World-without-end-hurled, heavy, heavy eyes."

So—till the final owl-car's yellow glare
Extends to foot its stair
Elongating your bones to people in
Everett, Malden.

Oh be enough awake then if you can
To press bell for the cemetery stop
(Or plod five blocks if you go by that gate),

Then the short street where no house shows a light
And snoring is not heard,
Up the plank walk that bumps beneath your tread
And home, and never, never speak a word.

Concerning the Human Image

Men who have seen
The human image in the Shakespearean glass
Distinguish Xerxes from Leonidas.

And though their mouths are stopped and shouted down
Hear more clear for that the hollow groan
Raised by the javelin of Laocoon.

And if they walk on pavements of no sun,
What's that to you at the world's ringside, releasing,
Bulletin by bulletin, the Dawn?

Sometimes renewed, but not by their own will
(Out of themselves only bad music still,
Shrill, grating, and—oh yes, you're right, afraid).

Yet they have seen the image Will descries
Shrug down Calvin's Hell, snap Cromwell's blade,
And grinning there at Marx in Paradise.

The Pool

This is the pool that Plato visited
In the late Indian summer of his year
To eat the golden honey harvested
By his own bees in June and July sun.

The stench and smothering out of the wick of our time
Blackens, cracks, and dries
The calm Madonna with Leonardo's eyes;
The rock she sits among
Waits in a bombsight to be otherwise.
She sees the falling leaves and dying leaves
That cling there still, or looking through the brown
Woven horror of the boughs, she sees
The empty, arching skull.

But things above still find their counterparts
Under this water: tree responds to tree
And hill to hill; the smallest flake that flies,
Glassed in the pool, finds as it falls its own
Minutest properties.

The numbered angels of Pythagoras
Pressing upon us from the upper air,
Marrowless, cold—how should they speak us true?
But in the pool, ugly or beautiful,
All are compact of pity and of fear
As we are, only real.

Forty O'Clock

It hardens, time hardens, the light,
The heart hardens. It is forty o'clock.

Poe's luminous forehead struggling in the gross
Bushes of memory
Bodily sensations of loss
Inability to tear off the burning
Garment of invisibility.

From lights in spring that tremble over water
Take endless trains in subways. Learn to know
The faces underground.
Where else shall love be found?
Or Hart Crane's face but where he once saw Poe?

The old man in the park feeding squirrels and pigeons
Is not by them regarded with suspicions.

O parks, night streets, dim shops, and then the door
Where children's eyes more beautiful than **blue**
Water without shadow
Shine and shine and shine and do not **know**.

Here where the world's variety grows narrow
The first fruit (or the last, if none should follow)
Is found in tangled grass, the puckering taste
Of getting used to slowly becoming a ghost.

Art and Logic

Logic is a thing like steel rails,
Straight, with death at the end,
Or like Freud consigning Europe to the bow-wows
Unless the myth he forged from his own fate
Make Europe turn again.
But in non sequiturs like mummy wheat
Or green toads sealed in ancient concrete,
Art begins where contradictions meet.

Inventory

Now I have lain upon too many beds,
Intent, unsleeping, with wide-open eyes
Waiting a splitting open of the sky
That does not come. No easy symmetries
Could take me—agile life on anxious earth
Makes music bright as pewter in Dutch kitchens
Crumple, melt, and blacken in the heart.
Only what I could see from where I stood
I wrote about, and all I count good
Is no more than the leavings of a mouse
In a huge, dark, uninhabited house.

The Patient Ones

The patient ones, if they can keep a friend,
If they can love, if they can only sleep,
If they can only keep
Quiet, and with their brows
Furrow the air like prows
Toward whatever shipwreck waits them in a minute,
Shall squeeze out the last drop of meaning in it,
But they must keep as quiet as they can,
For words are dreadful to a quiet man
Except such speech
As courtesy may teach.
Thus, while they are in time, blind hopes will rise
To nourish them and all their days will pass
Quietly, waiting a hypothetical spring,
And while they foot it on
Under blank skies or over burning stone,
Like crickets in the Valley of Dry Bone
Sometimes they will sing.

The Free

The poor have houses that are wondrous gray,
Color of wind and rain,
Color of woodsmoke on October days
When the last leaves come down.

And they have hands and eyes
That touch nor see not what they dream upon,
And in their yards and in their houses lies
All rubbish that the world is tired of.

And so Necessity, the rag picker
Who has no liberal views,
Bargains beneath the clotheslines in their yards,
And they alone have power to pick and choose.

Crusoe

Whenas from rocks the mist unblooms and clears
Crusoe awakes upon the strand, the shore
Where ships return no more.

His lifted eyes discovering no trees,
He thinks how many days, how many years
Piercing as nails shall mortify him here.

Accept, O Lord, this bottle of his tears.

The supernatural rigor of this land
Is nullified by neither curse nor song;
Nor can the greenest parrot's loudest squawk
Shelter the mind from the eternal rock
And bones of creatures gnawed and thrown away.

And it is tongueless being castaway.

And while his dusty head turns gray, burns brown,
He will think wistfully how sailors drown,
And being time's deepest scholar, study well
Every unwatered word beneath the mind,
And he will write it down
That after after there is after still.

Anglo-Saxon

King Alfred sensed among his country's words
England's destiny;
But Caedmon, rapt, among his master's herds,
Felt all their history:
How all men, once, had owned a common tongue
And clumsy dialects the wide world over
Remembered music that the first had sung,
And would discover,
Through cries confused, the excellent, true stem
And scattered vowels of Jerusalem.

Entry into Jerusalem

Under the billows where their bowl went down
The Three Wise Men of Gotham rub their eyes
To see in coral to the watery skies
The towers of a most impossible town.

On pavements that their knowledge proved a fraud
They enter softly, hiding their disdain,
That shallow persons should succeed again
And anthozoans be the Sons of God.

El Greco I

See how the sun has somewhat not of light
Falling upon these men who stand so tall;
See how their eyes observe some inward sight
And how their living takes no room at all—
Their passing stirs no air, so thin they are—
Behind them see small houses with small doors;
The light comes from an unfamiliar star
That lights their walls and falls across their floors.
What shall we say when one of these men goes
Into his house and we no longer see
His eyes observing something that he knows?
And if their houses brim with radiancy
Why does no light come through as those doors close?

El Greco II

The Greek began where color ends, with black,
And wooed the spectrum from the heart of night,
And though sometimes he trembled and turned back,
Painted as near as mortals do to light.
He knew that pictures for the ages' wear
Are not by tender colors hatched and nursed,
Nor pay the reckoning of time and air
Unless they stood on darkness from the first.
The Greek began with things that make men grieve:
The heartbreak and the certainty of night,
But in the very midst could still believe
And on his canvas generated light
Like the great sun that on so black a thing
Maintains the tall, blue, catholic sky of spring.

Lincoln

Something he trusted in us, and we fed
On his idea and held it in our mind;
His faith grew true through our love of him—dead;
And none dared touch the charged circle—his mankind.
But the machine was there and its demand:
What could we do but feed those jaws for pay
When there were no more prairies, no free land?
Yet, in the end, we thought, we'd go Abe's way,
Prove he was right—no need for any alarm—
And stay ourselves, though we were wheels to wheels
Whose steel teeth grate the rhythms of shop and farm
Down to an iron throb that never feels,
Or feels as useless friction, flesh and blood's
Parity and Lincoln's platitude.

Belphage: A Biography

Belphage wrote well, and from the top of his mind
Reported incidents and appearances.
Profound, significant, charitable, resigned—
We thought he could not alter. Entrances
Were made in him by care in his fortieth year.
He wrote no more because he would not carve
Personal sorrow into prose. The fear
Grew up in us that even Belphage could starve.
Almost he did, but in the interval
He was a child for wonder; as his brain
Grew leaner he perceived as comical
The explanations comfortable men maintain,
Saw holding up the rational facade
Nothing but angels, laughed, believed in God.

An Honest Magistrate

Picture of an honest magistrate
sifting the wheat from the chaff of what they said
In the case of the vanishing Jew the night before
   Passover:

The stone on the tomb, it seems, weighed nearly a ton
And made enough noise as it fell to waken the dead.
The guard report it pitched them onto the ground
And they found the stone five feet from where it
   had stood.

A spiced napkin, supposed to have wrapped the head,
They found carefully folded, separate
From the other cerements.
                        Common robbery?
Mystification to confuse the scent?
Calmly to prepare for the event?

He seems to have risen alone
With time and to spare, but he must have had help with
   the stone.

Sonnet for Redheads

Red hair is dangerous; it goes deep in,
Feeds at the central fire and so must burn,
And as men who work at ovens and furnaces turn
White, not red, your redhead has white skin.
And though the heat of the sun is crueler
To them than others, burns them, freckles them,
It cannot change their white to swart or dim
The holocaust reflected in their hair.

Nero and Socrates and Lancelot
Will witness this, and Antony's sharp queen,
England's eighth Henry, great Elizabeth,
Blake, Verlaine, Villon, and—take one more breath—
Shaw, Beatrice, Cesar Borgia, Magdalene,
Christ, William Shakespeare, and Iscariot.

The Positivists

The old like brown leaves crisp and cling
To what on earth may nearest lie;
All things which the adventurous mind
Finds out turn doubtful by and by,

But what is here because it is,
Because sere fragile fingers feel
Against them this, the old men say
That this is wisdom and no lie.

But in the silence where they toast
Dry toes beside a failing fire
The young man frets within his ghost
And shines his shoes and combs his hair.

Elegy for "Slim"

He will mount Jacob's ladder saw in hand,
Sucked cigarette between oblivious lips—
Not mortal now—through cutting out despond
Eternal to his tar-stained fingertips.

Hands that cut off dead limbs to save live trees,
Eyes that perceived death's shapes in the Argonne,
Feet that with whiskey's aid for twenty years
Climbed elm trees through annihilation

Now at the very top of that tall tree
That shadows all the world, but bears the sun.

The Mole

When the mole goes digging
He never meets a soul;
The stars are inattentive
To the motions of the mole.

He digs his frantic tunnel
Through chalk and clay and slime
His never-ending tunnel
A mouthful at a time

Alone; no planet bothers
To tell him where to dig,
For moles are very little
And worlds are very big.

And when his tunnel ceases
The little mole lies stark,
And at his back is dimness,
And at his head, the dark.

So to the mole all honor
And the labors of the mole,
With doubtfulness for tunnel
And ignorance for goal.

Farewell to the Wind

It fell upon the street and shook the house
And shook it like a rat, in pure fun.
I knew it was for me the wind had come.

We met beside a river. The night was dark
Save for one light on the other side of the water
That tangled with the water
When the wind flung upwards the plunging branches
        of trees.

I did not speak but sat on a bench by the river
And smelled the Red River
And autumn in August, and I watched the trees
Giving themselves whole to the wind's will.

(But mine was not the wind's, and moved in me
As when a man in a strange country
Encounters, not a friend, but the child of a friend.)

Then the wind spoke to me
Flinging a great arm across my shoulder,
Saying: You seem older;
Yet you are Mayo still, and I am he
Who shook a door once till you woke and came,
And we climbed to the top of Waite's Mount in a
        thunderstorm
And wrestled together in the roaring rain.

And after the long heat of the Bahamas
When your shoes were tight and your mouth confirming
        death
I slammed back the shutters of the dining room,
Chairs over tables, dishes over the floor,
With a puff of my breath,
And we walked all night together along the shore.
Sand stung your cheeks, and foam,

And my voice rose like an organ in the cathedral
Of human life, blowing the chorale
Of victory in the teeth of the world's pain.
Now we are met again.

What could I do? Hunched on the bench by the river
With his hand on my shoulder
Whose laughter lives forever?

Wind—I said—
Breaker of ties, breaker of promises,
Glad would I let your grasshoppers attend
The weedy garden of my daily bread,

But I have chosen of late
This people for my people
And their fate is my fate.

You are the shaker of the earth's four corners
And winnow them one by one,
But you cannot shake or winnow the four corners
Of my stone heart, and in those cluttered corners
Humbly, by accident, my work is done.

His arm leaped from my shoulder. He was gone,
Yet paused at the bend where the trestle crosses the river
To cry out thrice for scorn upon my end—
I had known that this was the way it would end
That first night on the hillside in the storm
But not that one day I should look upon
This wanderer as the beautiful child of a friend.

Metamorphosis

My shadow strides ahead and towers before me.
It is a most portentous-looking shade.
Is this the man my mother thought to have made
Before the truth came squalling and she bore me?
Look closely: Does it wear a coat of brown?
And brown shoes? spectacles? and need a shave?
Then it is surely me. I think we have
Changed places under this El Greco moon.
I am my shadow now and he the man,
And being chained to him I have to trot
After those heavy steps that tramp and tramp—
Now shrinking up, a pygmy African,
Now Gulliver, the slave of Lilliput;
But I'll be night when he puts out the lamp.

No Ghost

There is no ghost climbing by wavering lines
To aid you; under earth there is no eye
Follows you; at your birth
Only Death, your Death that knows this house,
Took thought for you, stood ready to assist
Delivery from all your mother bore,
Nor held, nor hurried you, as if to say:
"Will and take your fill and then I may,
For what is flesh itself but my door?"

The Angel

Eden was every man to me
Before my eyes had learned to see,
But when I sought their secret place
I met an angel face to face—
An angel with a flaming sword
In each man's soul stood up on guard,
To fend me off both night and day
And fend my burning love away.
I did not know the angel's name
In days when my young heart took flame,
But now I know it—or can guess—
The angel's name was Loneliness.
I love her better than I did
For now she keeps my secret hid,
And if she kept me out before
Now she keeps others from my door.
The broken shoes of indolence,
The mantle of deceit, the sense
Of soft threads weaving day by day
A certain web a certain way—
These are my own; no man may see
The unspeakable and secret me.

Iron Gate

To pass the thirtieth year is but to be
Other than one expected, barer here
The heart is than it was in many a year,
No longer cluttered with bright privacies.

Here Solomon perceives he is not wise
And with an eye upon the second prize
Divides desire with possibility;

Sometimes will talk with sailors of the sea
Because the sea gull in his proper breast
Beats louder now against a thinner door;

Lives now by miracle, and living tests,
In quiet desperation, by the clock,
The shifting shadows on the changeless rock,
But cannot guess what evening they portend.

He tries all things except the way to mend.

And since his certitude not always beams,
Snatches the shining runners as they fly—

Where nothing shall have nothing to repent
Even the awkward song is excellent—
And he has heard the thunder through his lie.

The Questioners

The sad sage-gray Dakota hills
That stood around me at my mapping table
Pestered with flies stay with me; the great
    moaning
Of wind that walks that country day and night—
The years of famine and the years of blight
Are in that wind, and all the helpless anger
That men defrauded turn against themselves
Before they lift their rifles from their shelves.
And I have seen the ghosts of the Dakotahs,
Out of revenge on white men, smut the corn,
Ride like Russian thistles on the dust storm,
Crack earth with drouth, as hoppers darken
    the sun.
And I have heard the foxes on the hill
Barking a question; insects at the sill,
Drawn by my lamp, as they flung themselves at
    the flame,
Whirred with their wings no other name but
    my name.
I have stepped from farmhouse kitchens and
    been drowned
In the great empty of the country nights
And seen the Northern Lights
Beam after beam shoot over, seeking me.
But I would not be found, and would not cry
"Here! Here am I! Send me!"
Or whisper from the ground,
For I knew I could not answer such hard
    questions
And better never heard and never found.
And yet I never cease to ponder the questions
Of the creatures of the country without trees,
But all the answers I know are wordy or bloody,
Sick with swords or social disease;

And though my country silence answered nothing
And vigilance and patience are unsure
I have given my love to the askers of hard
        questions
Till what discovers darkness finds dark's cure.

Sonnet for the Season

The erstwhile rich green earth growing barer now
And bushes all transparent; I can see
Precious little left for you and me
In fields where promise withered row on row;
And that is why details leap forth and stun,
Though there before; the foliage being gone,
Right through the ribs of that vast skeleton,
Once all the world, we see this different one.

Come! Through the ribs with you! Already here,
I sniff the funny air, groping your hand;
And I can see a thing from where I stand
Who can believe in six months of the year?
Yet here it is, and on my coatsleeve, too:
The first precise unerring flake of snow.

Ode

O early launched by terror into terror
To be in her gray eye a lonely runner,
Look in your own heart for her last answer:
"I," she replies,
"Am your own compromise."

One clean window were enough sky
To stand upright in but for compromise,
This evening in things, sifting
Into the brain like sleep, smoothing
Contrition and anger
Till they are only slumber
Under the sun and bones under a hide.

O Eye propped in the shade
To see the race the lonely runner made,
Caryatid, cajoler of days,
Foster nurse, beguiler of all sense,
Precise in consequence,
Double, and twin, Nature, receive man's praise.

The Oaks

All we know is there
And all we cannot know because the mind
Is shaped to no such knowledge, and I turn
Homeward at evening from my quarries there
To see you sitting by the window, or
Facing the windless trees through the glass in the door.
I cannot speak
Of these things any more, cannot say,
See, they are gone; this is a holiday.
But one will turn a page and there will be
Scrub-oak branches twisted every way
And turn another, wondering to see
The same branches under the same sky.

The strong laboring wings of birds
Return through the still air
And it is spring so far as spring occurs
Where these oak trees are.
Who would have guessed that only we, we two
Should ever know these oak trees through and through?
Or know the true, secret name of the river
That curls beyond them through brown mist or blue?
Or that tall tower on the other side of the river
With one small window and no visible door?

The Phoenix and the Turtle

Supposing all imaginable good
Accessible, and our living eyes could see
Unscalpeled of the gray prenatal film,
Where should we find it, think you, here at home?
Maeterlinck's bluebird by the kitchen sink?
Or boding in the light of summer sky
Apocalyptic with the thunderstorm?
Surely some sigh that rises and departs
Departs toward this? Some sensitive pulse in your wrist
Throbs faith at mention of felicity?
But when you hold the delicate fluttering creature
Dissonance comes, and the thing you held in your hand
Fades like the last cry that the winds take over
From some lost swimmer swallowed from the eye
In the gray, sucking sea's deformity.
Felicity is not for you and me;
And saying this with quiet level eyes
Calm on each other's faces, we shall be
Living creatures moving through the dusk
Distinguishing the seagull from the sea.
And we shall view the world with accurate eyes:
The sparrow's small voice quickened by the rain,
The contemplation in the mourning dove's
Four level tones will speak more nearly to us.
And what shall be whatever we do or say
We shall not know, nor know the imaged sky
We people with dying memories of the dead,
But confident in knowledge of the black
Rough rocks of this world, we shall keep our eyes
Intent on actual landscapes while we keep
Our scrupulous hunger polished like a sword
Until we flesh it in the thing adored;
For Euclid lied, and in this crooked world's
Cruel political geometry
Only the accurate eye,

Agile, intent, patient in one desire,
Shall see, perched high upon a telegraph wire,
The Phoenix and the Turtle of content.

Sonnet

On the warm air the breathing branches keep
Company with sunlight through the leaves;
On the white house next door the shadows sleep
Through the long afternoon, and June reprieves
The mind—that ancient malcontent—from thought
Of what must be, of that harsh bugle horn
That cries of one more battle to be fought,
Friend from friend parted, lover from lover torn.
Myra, there sounds the horn, and my indenture
Was of my own hand's signing. I must go
Under this dappled light on new adventure;
None but ourselves shall guess or ever know
That in such parting only shadows part—
Leaf-shadows on the homestead of the heart.

Starlight Patrol

Eyeshine of God, the scorn of stars wears down
Impertinences of time, and we regard
Through nets of blood, the nerves' interstices,
Steel starlight piercing down.

Still, still on earth, the blood's dark river roars
Between us and our consummation;
There on the other bank, up there, so plain
They hurt like wounds, our treasure, love, and friend.

The end is mystery; until the end
Watch the windows blink out one by one,
The buildings harden, and the stars define
The harmless sleeping lineaments of Cain.

In the Tunnel

I knew I should be here
Oh long ago,
Saw myself sitting here, scribbling here
Ten years ago,
But when I get up and leave this tunnel
I do not know where I shall go.

Thunder, spark,
Whistle cleaving the night
Glittering procession of light;
Then doubly
Dark.

Without the occasional sound
Of wheels going round,
Of trains going through,
Whistle and bell,
I should not know where we were
I should not know
I should sleep too well.

But here by sad commuters compassed round,
In the long tunnel
In blown, foul air, awaiting the quickening sound
Of wheels going round, I have seen
Soiled paper, torn
Newspaper softly blown
Down the long tunnel, I have known
The vision of crumpled paper and cannot get home.

Prelude and Fugue

I

Ascending alone at birth between the great
And lesser lights, the planets being placed
According to plan,
To earth I came, on earth my body was
Delivered weeping; I had left my sword
In safe hands somewhere behind Aldebaran;
But coming alone like this
Without insignia to tell the man
I could not guess my lineage or name,
Despaired of vindication, set my mind
To quarry up the only hard stone
Here in the Middle Kingdom—
Harder than that of Michaelangelo's *Night*—
Called Time, and out of this to build my tomb,

My tomb and house to last, because no bomb
Could shatter work of the least artisan
In this tough medium.

II

You see the shaky scaffolding, the stuff,
The often halted gougings, all the blocked
Ugly first motions—sometimes see me hurl
My hammer in the corner and go out
To take the measure of the meaningless night—
And doubt me; and I doubt,
                    but coming back
I always see this fingerpost or sign,
See it without a light when nights are dark,
Upon it, THOSE ARE PEARLS THAT WERE HIS EYES:
And all I know and take for world and wise
Puts on a certain incongruity,
Rises at midnight through the face of the clock

Or on my way to work
Like sunlight on the faces of the slain
Moves like laughter, and the task is plain:

No peace for you or me or any man
But labor with hard stone in all between
The laying down behind Aldebaran
Of his good sword and taking it again.

The Shirt

Silence more deep than silence is before
The whistle of the midnight local; deeper
Closer and colder than the element
That is to darkest swimmers palpable,
Such silence; and such winds as ever blow
Down certain forked abysses have conspired
To weave for me the garment I wear now,
The shining shirt I dreamed of and desired.
The mind that stood aghast
The heart that beat so fast
To see what it had seen
Are fitted out at last;
I had not thought the universal tailor
Had such an eye, could make a fit so clean.
This is the shirt that the most pitiless storm
Could not prevent from keeping a man warm.
And none dare steal it—none!
Even the raggedest beggar would not plunder
This splendid shirt, though he should freeze to the bone.
Moreover, it is known.
Only the other day a man I know
Remarked upon it, found it food for wonder
That Hercules wore a very similar number
A number of years ago.

In the Web

What you desire not starlight nor tearose
Breathing at evening from the bush by the house
Tells, nor does the dialect of water
Hissing from the faucet or the hose
Gossip of your loss.

They keep your secret well until you die,
And as the colors of the evening sky
Burn to darkness down, each solemn color
That blesses you before it turns its shoulder
Is tacit with your ghost.

Huge as the night with stars above your house
These patterns laid on emptiness revolve
Beyond all searching; seeds you scatter strive,
Determined things, beyond the studious
Solicitudes of love.

This night and every night they dance in fire,
These patterns of the slayer and the slain,
And now a cock with half his feathers gone
Crows for a dawn he shall not see again
And cannot but desire.

Wagon Train

As pioneering children, when no rain
Made water brackish in the last canteen,
Went right to sleep, and just as seldom knew
When guns were cocked and ready all night through,
So do we ride the earth's revolving wheel,
Moving across what prairies, to what wars,
Against what ambush, eye does not reveal;
Nor do we know what loyal outriders
Swing on to clear our path across the plain,
But drift to sleep where canvas hides the stars
Of the long planetary wagon train.

1939

Tell me, daemon eyes that know
All that grows invisibly
About us, what it is that you
See that our eyes cannot see.

I see the vegetable years
The thicket in the thinking mist
Drip incredible black tears
Over an old romanticist,

See the great trees that tempered noon
Thicken and lean about a house
Where no dog barks and no light shows
Through the gross trunks and twisted boughs,

And hear a whimpering within
Granted permission . . . then the sound
Of grinding key and lifting chain

And now the baying of the hound.

To Urizen

Take off, take off that burning crown
Of moon and stars, O Urizen:
The burden and the mystery
Take off and lay all down.

Your reign is done: the smallest hand
Groping for touch in blacked-out street
Twitches the circlet terrible,
The neon robe falls at your feet.

There will be no more progresses,
No lords to let you in,
But cindered earth where your feet go
And blood where they have been.

You will be hunted from sea and air
Rooted from earth till the kingdom
Of mere bare animal alone
The wide world over, come.

And animals shall rise and cry,
"We humbled Urizen."
But Los shall take your one good eye
And so begin again.

Sooth for the Chancellor

(1939)

You who feel the texture of this time
By touch direct—and shiver,
Having seen certain horses eat each other
And one dead friend return,
Whether in company or solitude,
Be waiting for the one impossible sign,
Be waiting for the coming of the wood:
When the trees march, poor soldier, we shall see
Whether the cold that halters you at core
Will tighten as you struggle in that dawn
With the fighter who was not of woman born.

On the Student Peace Strikers
Who Went to War

They said they would not go and then they did;
Into the violent. It was very fine,
But then, we did not know
Why they refused, in the first place, to go.
And what metallic thing
Ticks under their coats as they return
We have yet to learn.

I Had Seen Death Come Down

I had seen death come down like smoke at night
Or rise like mushrooms—this was nothing new,
Had been arranged beforehand, and I grew
Accustomed to its presence, viewed the sight
As in my native country, moved abroad
Inspecting collapsed buildings, leaning walls,
Condoling widows, and at funerals
Commending children to the unknown god.

Then came the death unlooked for: in the skies
Bright sunlight; on the faces, every one,
Smiles to the quick, the straight look in the eyes,
Much music, lest a man should think alone,
And at each bridge game and on every phone
Nothing but friendship, cheer, and enterprise.

Transitional

Only between we live: nowhere;
And fair, high-hearted ones,
Who thought they would not stay here, stay here.
And our way outward from betwixt and between
Gets lost among the chimneys, through gray air
Rises columnar to the evening star
Eternal over incongruity.

O not by accident the paint turns gray
On these white houses or that money does
No more than everything for anyone—
In the amber of money lies beauty, the dead fly—
And none can check the scale of usury
That forms on damask lip and honest eye
Or the blood feud fought out in every alley
Of once upon a time with someday.

But since I shall not lust to say my say
Anywhere else or care what words mean,
Visit me, hard Muse, betwixt and between,
Armored well with pins of crooked fire,
To hook a remedy
Narrow as mother love, no heavier,
No stronger than the air,
And hands too deep for credible find me.

New Hypothesis

For the vast quietness between the stars
The ugly tables and the rickety chairs
Comfort us; and till the universe
Yawns in its sleep, and lo! we are no more
We shall explore—
Opening and closing yet the soft pine door—
The mystery of better and of worse.
We should expect no better, we suppose:
Slapped cheeks, the giggled laugh, the throes
Of after liquor teach us to expect
Hard laughter, the shrugged shoulder, neglect
In age; yet hungry, crooked, or remiss,
The knowledge of the the new hypothesis,
Cool in the stars, burns in our forehead bones:
That human life might be better than this.

The Uninfected

I saw a man whose face was white as snow
Come slowly down the mall,
And he was followed by another one
Till there were seven in all.

Now this is very strange that lepers be
Allowed to walk abroad in broad daylight.
I shook myself, and quickly turned to call
A bluecoat, and as suddenly caught sight

Of one in blue ruling the thoroughfare
Who made me passage through that brawling sea
With one raised hand. I spoke, and he inclined
To hear my word, the face of leprosy.

I turned and went straight on to search my own
Face in the next shop window mirror-glass—
Still no infection, not a single spot,
So I stood there and watched the lepers pass

Till four drove up to take me to a place
Where I live now, attended very well
By several strong male lepers dressed in white,
Eating what I like, sound as a bell.

The Forgotten Soldier

We too, it seems, possess
The wit to send the cylinders of war—
Enjoying to a man
The delicate partnership of hand and gun
To wing the rare and wary bird of peace.

Oh not for us the time
Of fiddles playing over in the pavilion:
We stood outside like gray
Wolves in the moon, then bedded for a dime
Or rode the rails into the West's vermilion.

Many a morning in gray waking streets
We learned what clubs were for,
And learned the use of stockings filled with lead
And have been left for dead—
In many an alley learned this art of war.

We have been students almost everywhere
Since hunger taught us wit.
We know war to the bone—
But of a peace that follows after it
We do not know and have not ever known.

In the Time of the Great Wind

Tonight the wind blows as it would blow down
The last tree, the last house, the last man;
Tonight the Allies leave Norway writhing
Like a cut worm under a boot stamped down.

All night planes in their scores keep laboring
From the new airport half a mile away,
And my heart labors with them, and the wind
Keeps blowing, blowing; this is the second day.

Now all the world grows insubstantial;
Only the wind exists, and it is steel
Scraping the world, and all not rooted well
Follows like old newspaper, comes to heel.

What will remain when it has blown its fill?
Not bread, not wine, not children's sticky hands,
Nothing, unless the hapless heart can wring
From wind, on wind, through wind its wayfaring.

They Say the World Was Weighed

They say the world was weighed
In golden scales a very long time ago
And tipped the beam; but now it is not so.
The fire is falling on America
And everything there is is straw, will burn.

Hurry, if you're only going through,
But if you stay, the thing is your concern.
No tea is in the harbor now, the tower
Shows not one light, nor two;
After this hour the fiery minister
And "Yes, sir! Yes, sir! Yes, sir! Certainly, sir!"

The Signposts

Airplanes will move across the raindark sky
  With healing in their wings;
Water will cool men's tongues when we shall lie
  Unknowing of these things.

Where we went wrong and could not find our way
  Back to the fork in the road
Signposts like pointing men will rise to say:
  "This highway is no good.

"Here travelers are changed; here they become
  Pillars of salt and stone.
Their minerals cry, 'Turn back, oh daughter, son;
  Take the appointed one!'"

To Catch the Common Face

To catch the common face which is all faces
The man whose name is Alpha and Omega
Calmly, as is his custom, paints the square,
The bombers zooming down, the thermit's roar,
The popcorn stand split open, the common face
As it was in the beginning and shall be—

Also, a quieter subject: boy with harmonica
Beside a girl in her mother's high-heeled shoes:
Their piping play, their growing pains, their mating—
Limns and gives each excellence its dues
Though these be all ignored in the every paper
And the boy's end be gas, the girl's the stews.

Day after day, among harmonicas,
Kisses, high heels, and money in munitions,
He circumvents the enemy's positions
And in this bloodstained, whistling shaft of stars
Follows the rare art as best he can
To catch the beautiful lineaments of man.

The Center Is Everywhere

The D Minor

Through what rock-strewn tunnels, O companions,
What wind-hurled clouds through passes in the mountains
You come!—sometimes moving overhead
And sometimes under, native to this ground

And natural guides over these rocks, but banished
By who knows what cabal
Of ancestors, atomic, integral
Who took this ground and mapped it and are dead,

And it is well with them. The map indeed
Is beautiful and firmly drawn; the wood
Withdraws resemblance, as the lines of a hand
Change gradually, to their promised land . . .

Twangings as of sweet stringed instruments
On lone traverses heard, or chat-birds
Always unseen by man by one man heard
In the dead-low and middle of the night

Speak, and the shiver of responding blood
Speaks the companion to the ancestor
Who Procne-like in his dry forest-bed
Cannot speak again; his children

Blinkered, plated well with eyelid-scorn
For what is not according to plan, hold on
To what there is of love like contraband;
And so the banished ones

Infiltrate the sad ranks: For one a door
Opens in singing sun; another hears
Marching and counter-marching to a drum
At earth's core; and one you sleep beside

Mutters in sleep: "Bridegroom, behold your bride."

Old Knifedge

"Causes are not to be multiplied beyond the necessary."
—WILLIAM OF OCCAM

Don't say, "It is beautiful."
To what proud god, William,
Could sacrifice be better than Old Knifedge
Who splits hairs with precision?

But I know a god, Will, that's crueller:
Insanity, obscenity,
Billboards and headlines are
His angels through eternity,

For evil is a spirit, God knows,
Combining murder with profit,
Chopping up Chinamen's chances like old clothes
Being made into a carpet,

And that steep place leading down into the sea
Is Objectivity, and perched thereon
Old Knifedge waits his opportunity
To split the hair the sword is hanging from.

A Call from Leviathan

Instanter, like a flash of heat-lightning
Forked four ways for claws, continuous
Beyond my scrap of garden, Leviathan
Smiles over the fence in the rain.

The whatnot on the mantel
I won at the country fair—how it trembles;
Where's the grin
Of my sociable little dog who danced him in?

And on his knees behind the henhouse, who
Shuts my rooster's cock-a-doodle-doo?

Iron School

Hobbes, Locke, Descartes and all
Who reared the shining intellectual
Dyke against the daemons of the heart—
Our unacknowledged legislators—heard
A trumpet in their heads, and then occurred
Buckle of brick, sea-water over steel,

And in the rush of daemon after daemon
Saw themselves as air-currents in air
Or water poured in water; as they shrank
To roof, stack, tree from the black tossing ink
That carried chairs and tables, eyes and hair
In one black mixture to the common sink,

Recollection of themselves appeared
Arbiting all with eyeless, abstract hands,
And this one leaped for fear, and this for pride,
But some clung stubborn, though the height was chill,
And while cocks crowed to usher in false dawn
Matriculated in the Iron School

Where dealing with the sea's pandaemonry
And heart's affliction is the prime study,
And History tide-marks showing how high
The last flood rose, and Science the thumb-rule
That mystery swills all, and he who knows
What he does not know is least the fool.

The Bowl

There was a certain Zero, and he was
A listener at night to children's cries
And so grew witness to the open space
At center of all such peripheries

Where swims a goldfish in a narrow bowl—
Six colored pebbles and a glaucous weed
For all the world, the daily crumb of bread
Drifting from somewhere down to his mouth-hole.

This is the size of it. "But not the praise,"
Los replies, attired in gray and rose
At the East window, "I at once assay
Nothing and all: goldfish in goldfish bowl
And I in my blue "O" alike assume
A great reckoning in a little room."

86

"Whose Center Is Everywhere"

Shaped, colored, given form
(Says the Philosopher)
By our own eye, the blue sky arches down
To land and ocean, houses, ships, and men,

Dawn defining like Angelico
Castle, sail, and pebble in the road
With its own *haeccitas*, the hard, blue
Eternal bounding line.

Familiar, comfortable,
There is my cow, and there
My emerald corn glittering in the sun,
But look straight up and all

Slides toppling; granite hill
Reels drunk to the horizon; treetops stare
Vertiginous and of two minds; and one
Is to let go;

The other, though,
Is to cling on, seeing clear
It is meridianed and centered by
The pure blue, the apple of its eye.

So cow, so dog, so pebble in the road:
The center is everywhere,
And if I grope toward the periphery,
Roll earth into a ball that shrinks away,

I'm at the center still,
And Icarus and thrown Bellerophon
Glimpsed no circumference through their long fall
But cartwheeled at the center through it all.

Oracle

I am just on my way tomb,
Several voices calling different things,
Such as, "Is it better to be kings
Without doms?" or "How,
Having climbed clear to Abstraction
To get back to our throne?"

Knowledge is ice-crystal-wonderful
Raised on nothing upwards into cold—
And by what thievery? Who plucks up whose

Brains who has it? Will he keep it? You
Whose eyes' blue vacuum draws whirling in
More than heart can know, do you think so?

Does it make us more royal? You can tell
Who bathed in Shelley's radioactive
Contaminated waters once, and heard
The death-boy crying from the Renaissance
"Never repent!" till B-14's like robins
Covered the children up in the deep wood.

Weep for yourselves, for them. But do not weep
For the New Men, They keep
Counsel on every level, dream, believe
Only this oracle: *Drink/air   eye/light*
Touch/fire tongue/water   greet occluded rock
With speech so large stars knock,

And though your speech be all
Honey and locusts to the general
Obsessed with mountains and space still for doubt,
Though they pile up mountains over mountains,
Speak! Who hear you crying in their mountains
Shall be torn like mandrakes, shrieking, out.

Fiscal Year: A Report

The up-ended truck on the embankment,
The luck of the non-elect
Attest the fiscal year's
Risus sardonicus, the tight fit
Of things around the heart.

To lie on a beach in the sun,
To walk with a friend a summer afternoon
Talking sense into things
Was not in the memorandum; nevertheless
We minded our own business.

It was a funny business: overhead
The doves but half concealed
Atomic preparations; under floor
The sharp-toothed pioneer
Counselled a new start:

An open season with an open heart;
But his was hardly one.
And we who have worked so hard and gone so far
To be invulnerable say
The whole business of being invulnerable

Seems in a very bad way.

A Reassurance

"By heaven, he echoes me
As if there were some monster in his thought . . . "
OTHELLO, III i.

The swollen legs and ankles, and the slow
Growing contentment that it should be so
In the apposite season, give us
The customary smile that always now
I give to you, you me.
Within us moves a purpose and a power
Not ours, nor ours to question; waiting here
We feel the appointed and fulfilling hour
Vulsive in China and Siberia
Converging on
Moscow, New York, London.
Sick in the mornings sometimes, but the nausea
Wears off by noon. Preoccupation
With liquefaction falling on our world
And theirs in an eyeblink makes us less insane
With private dreams, and food tastes excellent
Eaten against the vertiginous event.
(Smile)
Take my hand
(Smile)
It will be all right.
You can't unthink, you can't unlink again
The Hiroshima chain. Our marriage rite
Was the bridal of the earth and sky.
Accept the irreverse, consign, resign
Yourself wholly at the first pangs
Into the expert hands
Of Doctor Deathandnight and bring, bring,
Bring this monstrous birth to the world's light.

Nausea

How late the assassins ply their trade tonight:
The air is sweet with corpse-breath, and the slight
Shivering of trees in starlight
Whispers death in nature. The old order
Changes, giving place to murder,
Peculiarly by air—
Yet all my Lady's thoughts are centered here—

Here where above the city, on a girder,
Hamlet, his feathers ruffled in disorder,
Talks with his father's ghost. He tests the bare
Dissyllable, "Revenge!" but on the stair
Descending to the pavement and the heat,
Where, under towers, ten thousand tired feet
Beat, rebeat, grows ill and is sick in the street.

Still my lady in her silver chair
Feels to its last minute particular
And sickening core the mystery of war.
She sees Prince Hamlet choose his rapier
Perpetually, and from her parapet
Above this world cries out with infinite
Heat: "Get about your business, Paraclete!"

Sonnet

The earth that lets us in is soft as fern;
The sky that bars us out is hard as rock:
It has no knob to twist, no hinge to turn
And knuckles bleed upon the slightest knock.
Earth, then! Never look back. The sky's flare
Is Sodom, salt to you. Earth's mountains rise
Steep to foothills down till pastures bare
Teeth of stone at singed refugees.
You in your hat and coat! (gone, gone
The homestead where you put them on) take
What lies nearest—a book, a gnawed bone;
No souvenirs, no photos for God's sake!
The sky, a vortex passed already, leans
Hunched above us, waiting what earth means.

Held Moon

Wind there was none; only a breeze came by
Sniffing about it for a place to die
And found some leaves and died; on the gray lawn
Piled leaves said nothing until trodden on.

Then I saw the moon
Held like a ball of steel in a pair of pliers
Or a pale wrestler by another wrestler
Scissored, in the crotch of the dooryard elm.

And it was pinched and gaunt as Yorick's skull
To no stars at all bearing witness
That, viewed through human eyes, at a certain angle,
The moon may come to this.

The Lady and the Tree

I saw a tree take root in a lady's hand
And deep into the marrow of her bones
Grow, coil, and feed. The lady suffered.

The moon is a light. The sun is a light. The eyes
Are not light but a well
That sinks down into what will pleasure us.

Maizie Goldenhair was harvested this morning
In bins and silos her sweet kernel's stored;
But underground, tangled with thoughts and bones

The roots consume; the lady weeps and mourns.

Cat

Raise or depress your eyebrows at a cat,
The cat sees just as clearly in the dark:
And cat is cat whatever anyone
Thinks and loves to sleep in the sun and claw
Cloth and lift eyes like jewels for
Admiring connoisseur
And steal and kill with de-
Liberate cruelty, whether you will
Or no, eyebrows or no eyebrows.

The Thief in the Night

He comes like a thief. Not moonlight—this alone
Explains the way he was and was not there
In places where the trees were all cut down
And nothing cast a shadow, heard the prayer
Of treetoads pleading for their ancient cover,
And stole, where pasture brush was all burned over
And not a rabbit nibbled in the black,
Furtive by moonlight, and the seed of clover
Took root, grew green, and brought the living back.
But now, though moonlight shines as bright as day
On silo, barn, barbed-wire, and apple tree
And in the ground-mist lilacs feel as warm
As rich clothes long worn and just thrown down,
In the flick of an eye, he is here, he is there, he is gone.

Ice Storm

Because each oak tree is encyst in ice
The leaves hang down like fruit; the bushes are
Fountains rising toward the central spout
Of one glass-clustered willow. So the stir
Of mist through dripping branches all night through
Put on eternity. We neither knew
A trumpet blew nor felt the whole earth shake;
Yet children playing with the evidence
That soul is form and does the body make
Wake us with their shrill cries: the news is true:
The forms of things endure and glister through.

Nightpiece With Skyscrapers

Steamy late July
Finds me beside this voiceless inland sea
Perched on a skyscraper at night; the night
Obscures the poverty.

Here rise the Ozymandian cliffs, and here
People live and sleep and work inside
Shapeless thighs of anonymous deities;
And some have leaped from here like sterile seed.

So Tannhauser, whom I knew very well,
Also climbed a hill to get to Hell—
And she who has a mirror
For every single atom of her skin

Was involved, as I remember.
But here she has no shrine
Unless these cromlechs try
To get with child the inconceivable sky.

The Fair Bargain

Sad, impecunious, tortuous deity,
Miraculous wine maker, fisher from air,
Wash my foul feet, but hurry, hurry—
I lose thirty drachmas if I am not there.

"*Quickly.*" Through black streets I rush to the issue;
Dim in the spider-priest's web they await
But a word, a look—"Here he is! Take him!"
To chink in my palms and fill up my plate,

For I have loved gold and I have loved silver
More than mother or father or girl of the ways,
For they are as eddies of air, and as faithless
But money is certain, and money repays

The affront of his knowing that I would be doing
What I knew I should do from our very first meeting.
It seems now I need not have grinned to redeem him,
Nor need, even now, bring this last kiss of greeting.

Yet I shall bring it, for money in pocket,
And he will return it who knows what I do;
Just is the bargain where both parties profit.
Buying and selling what they wanted to.

The Sad Photographer

I

It seemed to him that he had lived to now
Through some oversight of the manager.
This filled him with inordinate and shame-
Less inner certainty that he must show
The slant of the dead on what the living do

If only to keep faith with the mangled body
(His own) that was not found in the ravine
Under the railroad trestle, or that other time
Monoxide smothered in a hotel room—
Blue face (his own) among the magazines.

And he was seen in many a dead-end street
As the first milkman jingled out his cart;
As hawkers in the public streets cried out
He lifted images from their dead eyes
And printed them upon the public gaze.

Then the Greater Fabricator came
And haled him, grasping tightly his free arm,
Out of a counting house, resonantly pressed
A bundle of broken mirrors on his chest.
He had arrived; he was a public man!

II

"A definite aid to the psychotic," one doctor said;
Another was heard to insist from coast to coast:
"You who cannot afford an accredited psychoanalyst,
Behold the man!" He knew then that he had lost
His battle with Enemy; the Enemy

Had employed the feminine strategy
Of absorbing the thrust at a weak point and then
Folding around the adversary.
"How stark!" they said, "How tragic!" "What subtle humor!"
To every vivisected carcinoma.

His bone especially was much commended
As being more sensible than the stock article;
Some said, "One actually hears it *rattle!*" and some
Gnawed it publicly with a wreath to the owner.
Nothing was left the sad photographer

Short of the resurrection of the dead—
A lost and difficult art, and yet he said
"Lazarus, come forth!" but Lazarus
Does not stir, and so he says again:
"Lazarus!" and yet again, "Lazarus!"

Saucer (Flying)

It follows that the vision is hard to describe. For
how could a man report as something different
from himself, what at the time of his vision he
did not see as different but as one with himself?
—Plotinus

That streak of light that ebbed and flowed
About the cloudy midnight sky
Was not a bug, was not a star,
A plane, or anything his eye
Could classify officially.
Officially it was not there,
But lying on his back, a pipe
Clenched in the corner of his jaw
He saw it skitter all around
Like some bewildered meteor
Homeless on earth, homeless in air
Or if not homeless, bound beyond
Local accommodation.
He shrugged, knocked pipe out, and went in.
But lying in his naked bed
He knew he would not sleep alone
Again. The spirit of the age
Had found a place to lay its head.

Life Ended of a Sunday

Life ended of a Sunday in my town,
And in the churchbells you could hear the voices
Of heavenly monitors.
On Monday you began where you left off.

But now between a Saturday and a Monday
Sundays have got lost; we cannot tell
The difference between churchbell and firebell
And messengers from heaven

Visit us on weekdays as they can
In shirtsleeves or anything,
Knocking us down like ten-pins, hit-and-run.
And this not knowing when

The next Visiting Angel will come in
Without even knocking or ringing the bell
Makes us pale. If living
Never ends, how can it begin?

Black Man

Under the incense-bearing tree, the barkers
Set up their wares, and many are the takers,
And one cries "Hurry!" and another "Please!"
And then the bareback riders, the cute dancers,
The tired walkers, the lost children's cries.
Out of girls, gun-galleries, cigars
Who can lift, pluck, pluck clear out, his eyes?
And who is this Black Man
With holes in his head for eyes and nose so fine
His nostrils scent the incense-bearing tree
Here on the asphalt where our feet sink in?
Hot is the sun. Who is this Black Man?

Magazine Stand

What are all these magazines shuddering for?
Whose idea of beauty-wonder-terror
Mirrors here? The fear that we shall smother
Goes back to the birth-trauma
But not this mouth-watering
Relish in the belly for pure fear.

Look at that cover.
It is a forerunner.
There never was a dream did not come true.
Killer, Satyr, Sadist, Social Pillar,
Rockwell Rube, Far-Star-Traveller,
What are they doing, what are they doing to you?

Elegy for a Black Bird

Only in terror could you take delight,
Bird solitary and colonial,
And that bad laughter at the dead of night
At the lake's edge is thine
At all those ply-wood cabins on the shore—
Rotten planks under. If the wages are
Death for estrangement, what need you fear more?
And whose estrangement is it now, I wonder?

Student of weird, knowing catastrophe
Before the white light and the blazing blank.
No check upon America's gyre, but still
A lucid moment and a prescient
At brink of the abrupt; frequenter of
The billboard-hidden, the forbidden fen—
No Bulfinch-Greco-Roman-
Temple—First-National-Bank American.

Above the mean streets and the gaslit square
You looked upon the house our fathers reared
And saw the crack that crept from crypt to tower,
Cried out with none to heed
That Psyche had been sepulchered too soon
And heard her vault gape wide.
Now, though the dank tarn bubbles with green water,
Sleep on, Black Bird, sleep well, being justified.

The Two Worlds

Deracinate
The atom from its mate,
Travel by rocket to the last fixed star
And tell
Enlargement that its path is circular,
Call travel celibate.

You cannot tell how large love is from this,
For looking in its eye your mansion is
And all its distances
No farther than a handclasp from a hand.

From this and from the like build up your land
In space and time: Your stars will be the same,
The intricate processional ballet
Of night and day,
And all your waters Lethe at the end,

But where you set your fire
To wood on stone, through Dionysius prove
"The things below are as the things above,"
Depend upon it, both are two, and love
Makes one world ours and one the Enemy's
From here to the last star.

I Saw My Father

I saw my father rising through the air
Higher than State House, Bunker Hill, and all—
From kissing earth ripped to a sky of fear . . .

Once, with straight black hair,
He sweated blood, I've heard my mother say,
Until there came a knocking at the door,
Heavy, peremptory.   Nobody

Nobody was there.

Thereafter he grew gray
Gently, quietly. At night, the dream
Stirring the roots of his hair, he would cry out,
A minister who had received his call . . .

Would he have answered me had I called?
Chewing a piece of grass, I stood there
In his green field waving frantically
"Goodbye! Goodbye! Goodbye! Goodbye!"

I shall not find his equal anywhere.

Two Poems for a Child

I

Out of the sour sea-foam and from between
The crooked granite of the sea you come,
Wistful and venturesome,
To view the rigors of the scene humane
And taste of contradiction and of home.

Your guardian angel speaking to your mind
Will guide you into touch and into taste,
Corners of bookcases will be unkind,
Delicate fire bloom and air bequeathe
The varying odors of the world and wake

With every breath you breathe
With every joy by sleep not quite undone,
The selfless cherub, Contemplation,
With eye intent, Whose might is to possess
All that we can hold of happiness.

II

"Happiness!" We're caught before we start.
Your tongue and ears and eyes
Took the hook with your first sunrise,
And now it snags in the hair
You comb with so much care.

You nibbled and are caught
In a world, sweetheart,
Where fish grew birds, birds men
Before God let you in,
And must turn back to fish
Before you get your wish.

Pillar of Smoke

For Francis Bertrand McCarthy

I saw the bright smoke of the train before
I saw the train—the great white plume it wore
Stood supernatural, somehow of the sun,
Among the smokestacks of damnation
Raised by the Power Company. Up clay sky
It towered patiently while you swung aboard
And while we talked, and while
A ghost from limbo intimately known
Smiled, nodded in the aisle,

And it continued holding up the sky
While I waved to you at your window in the train
And when the grin
Froze on our faces at the turn of wheels,

And with the train block, bug, dot, nothing grown,
Still to the zenith upward on and on
This glittering pillar shone

Oh sky again so tall
That we can breathe and all!

Suddenly it was gone, but still the sky
Bore the impression, and firmament
Lifted from gray canvas to huge tent
Around this eddying, immaterial pole
Stood, and maintained itself, and did not fall.

Cavannah

Walking the path that led down by the brook
Before they bricked it in, I saw Cavannah
It was the same path that Cavannah took
Before they bricked it in; Cavannah looked
Like a mechanical exercise in Cavannah
Not drawn from life but drawn from memory
By lazy fingers that could not recall
What he had murdered and what kept alive
To be walking down this path again at all.

Passing, his eye met mine. He winked at me . . .
Under the swept brick, the trimmed trees,
The brook, sand-strangled, still—it could be—ran.
I write in hope and ignorance. What else,
Among time's ruins, could his winking mean?

The Silly Lovers

The silly lovers talking of nothing, and
Innocent of the innocence of the world
Of their knowledge—having forgotten again
All that it ever knew, it jollies them
Pretending it's not afraid
Of the new revelation, the new dispensation—
Think how the world will never again know two
Lovers so bone-certain, as they are,
That they can talk about nothing and pretend
To be like other lovers earth has known—
Knowing their difference . . .

Well, how does it end?
You certainly ought to know: it's your story.

There was a little wind blowing that day,
And as they came around the corner of an office building
They found that it had blown the world away.
There wasn't any world. They were alone—
And it didn't matter at all, it was wonderful!
Their happy ending came at the beginning,
Providentially, so that come the War,
Or a fall in the price of hogs, or being poor,
They would know how it ended before all.

Breathing Bridge

I

This is the Breathing Bridge that you must pass
Or cross (oh cross). Here there are many people—
First feelings, then thoughts, then people,
But the people are feelings still, and the feelings things
Hard to distinguish, undistinguishing.

II

You think you see a man
Horribly cut down,
And look again and see it is not so
But a great tree felled on a slope of snow,
And hear a voice say, "Now
Is the acceptable time."

(O pardon me, thou bleeding piece of tree:
In this dim light I thought you were a man.)

You see the carpenter
Arrive with square and saw
And nails to bind the wood

And in an hour it is a table spread
With bread and wine as though
To eat and drink were nobler than we know.

III

"He jumped off the Bridge, Officer!"

"He couldn't do it, Mister.
There's a fence on both sides a mile high."

"And yet how thin it is, Officer.
Thousands go through by way of fire and air—
How paper-thin it is!—oh, every day."

Then with a jerk of the thumb which does not explain
(For all farewells to you are actual);
"Through, Mister, but not off. The orders are
Returns for each detour,
Meeting departures, welcoming farewells.
Try it! Go on!
You'll find as he did
A table spread after that long climb,
And as you finish the last glass of wine
There'll be the Breathing Bridge stretching ahead."

City of Light

Come, let us go into the City of Light:
Silently now in the evening street-cars move
Along their gleaming tracks, the passersby
Drift at will, the streetlamps momently
Flatter and subsume the fading sky.
The shops grow magical and our desire
As high as to the chimney tops where one
Lately too much alone, a hermit crab
Clenched in the teeth of his integrity
And hung in air to dry,
Had a green vision of his element
And waking found it so. Come, let us go,
For music from a thousand juke-boxes
Spills from doorways and the shuffle of feet
Makes a profounder music. In the street
Spectres and Emanations long apart
Look, recognize each other, now it is dark.
It is dark now. Behold the City of Light.

Not Now? Not Yet? Not Here?

Not now? Not yet? Not here? Must we go on?

A little farther yet, my old blind friend.
Listen. Can you hear the wind in the pines?
Here we may rest a little without fear.
Here, when the dawns were clear of mist and rain,
Men have glimpsed the City . . . Sit down, sit down;
Feel with your hand how smooth the stone is worn.

Already darkness breaks between the peaks
Showing the ledge we perch on—God knows how—
And little else; yet men have seen it here.
De Quincey saw it once from here they say
Through opium's memory of the Good, and God
Showed to John at high noon terribly,
Bridge, River, Pillar, Tower unobscured;

No thunderhead or smoke of forest fire
Or streaming cloud as now to wall it in
Till Poe beheld as it were undersea
Thinking it drowned, and Mann in his despair,
Lost on the mountain, saw through driving snow
The City and the stain of human blood
That seared his pupils through the crystal wall.

But we see nothing, see no cloud unclose
And like so many after and before
Take bread and eat and get up and go on
To pass the corpses of far better men,
It may be, or to stumble on our own;
Nor weep; for many who have reached this ledge
And seen things clearer have gone blinder than you.

Here are the bread and cheese and here the wine.
Come, eat; the selfsame hour
Will find our feet descending. The wind now
Is as breath in the pines. A stream
Moves or seems to move down there. Oh blind!
Shining eyes which while I clacked the hour
Have seen the whole, Bridge, River, Pillar, Tower!

The Second Coming

A god shoots straight; we always miss the mind
And hit the man. But from the mouths of the suitors
There rose black smoke that blew to Hell and gone,
And innocent dogs licked their black blood like waters.

For that far-travelled man
King Ulysses left his bow behind
In Ithaca to rust with his good name
Caked with the salt rumor of the sea.

Over a stretched frame, Penelope
Pondered that great bow
Until she launched her heart as an arrow
After her Lord. The swift hands weaving

And unweaving the bright picture in the frame
Moved in a present absence across seas;
When gossips, suitors came
She was at home only by courtesy.

A dog, a swineherd, an only son
Saw through rents and windowed raggedness
The second coming; incredibly the armor
Of the quarreling suitors seemed to melt away

In their most need; and when the beggar,
The old, vile beggar in whose bowl they threw
Their orts and leavings, touched that vast bow
Innocent dogs had joy; but they, sorrow.

Letter to Karl Shapiro

Where Athanase once hankered for a star
There was bad odor; Poe's umbilical
Was never clean cut off: Virginia
Restless in tomb, Elaine unlovable
Supine in wandering barge, Beata in bed,
Smell similarly water-lily-bad,
And have you ever had to wash by hand,
When the machine broke down, a baby's diapers?

Virginia, Elaine, and Beata
Assuredly did not, and did not see
How such chores lead two ways: to the corrupt
Winding-sheet affected much by Donne
And to the swaddlings wetted in a manger
By one who bleeds through all the firmament,
There being more room there than there was at the inn
For word at once symbol and referent.

And such is poetry. Maybe we shall find
(Clawing through language till our fingers crack)
Blake's steel dividers drawing on chaos
Life's wiry line, or land in Rodin's vast
Hand squeezing succulent clay as many ways
As love has eyes or horror tongue to tell
Or see from Patmos on a blue Monday
Earth's last diaper hung in the sun to dry.

The Return of No-Man

Oh be sure,
For all your changes from the island kingdom,
Even in your own unurned
Ashes you return,
Turning, turning, leaving on many a shore
Carved stone or curious tale, Imagination's
Children in guilty time,
The Odyssey of all war did not kill.

Whether in rags on swollen feet you come
Or as the eagle swooping to retreat,
This shore will harbour you, guarded or no.
Go on—none will oppose—and in this place,
Entelechy to all your guile and toil,
Let slip the wrinkled mask from off your face
And on the faithful grass
Talk with Telemachus.

The old dog knows the beggar, who he is,
And dies knowing. The noise
(The toast goes round, the table in a roar)
Of suitors' groans shall be his obsequies.
Still in her clean bower the wife of wives
Weaves and reweaves the sexual tapestry
To gentleness, devouring years—and you
Stand up, strip off your rags, and bend your bow!

Your Sheet of Paper and Your Nightly Pillow

Your sheet of paper and your nightly pillow
Are your Bethesda-still
Pool, lame beggar, where
You watch for "angels" in the *lingua franca*

But in your native tongue
Nameless, for it is bad luck to name
The least shape that troubles these inane
Waters. When they come

Plunge in like log or boulder
Heedless of gasping lung and crimped limb,
These messengers had as soon pass through
You as through unspeculating paper,

The pillow's idiot news always the same,
But in the moment of the great procession
In your limbs they become
Feet assured, the rock-face of the mind.

A Recognition

A: Why do you lie, my friend
Like sea-weed in the sun
Here on the shingle?

B: And who are you who come with hooded eyes
While sun lets fall the steel and gold of noon,
Stupid with speculation?

A: Out of love to what I deem most true,
The ultimate cry of joy, desire's repose.
I walk upon the public beach to bring
A body to my hope's long suffering.

B: An hour ago, my belly full of sea,
I crawled up here with nothing in my hands
Except a single smile
Broken and instantaneous like lightning.

A: So it is you again. The rest will keep.

B: No, no; go on. For now I lightly leap
Up on your back and cling
I can forgive you almost anything,
Partly at least for thinking how my beard
Divides around your neck, the ends meeting.

A: In truth . . .

B: What else is really interesting?

A: I shall be grave as gravity again
With you upon me.

B: Therefore, my old friend,
Study philosophy and lightning—
Of habit's slaves the most inerrable—
For striking once and liking where it fell
It strikes again and again, like ritual.

Orpheus on B Deck

Muttering, blubbing, breaking,
Incessant lip on every moving prow,
Green and unquiet, hush now, listen now;
This is the sailor song that rules you.

Now a lewd and now a plaintive strain
Out of the Astor Bar, the Dirty Spoon
In Kingston or Nassau
Slip from the singer and his gray guitar

Enmeshing you, pale-eyed in the moon's ray
Invulnerable worm in triple mail
Whose map-imagined tail
Encircles all. They coil you in their coil.

Now league on league, nacreous, glittering,
Lift up your hissing head, and sway, and swing,
Take on the human face, the human form,
And dance, sea-serpent, to the sailor's song.

The Snake and the Eagle

The snake peers over my notebook—or is it my fingers
Supporting it as I write? Come, enter my song,
Wisdom. The self-contained
Furniture in the living-room will not share it;
All I have is your last cast-off skin.

Therefore go up and down and in between
Timber and underwood, go everywhere,
Detested or understood,
Snake-in-the-grass subtle beyond compare,
Until my eagle leap from his high cloud.

Colloquy

Because it is the mind and has its nature,
Because so little of the world is left it,
It will observe with interest, and accurately
The coming on of its own end. The fight
Is over; the triumphant earth, too ignorant
To know that it has triumphed, is drinking beer
At Tony's place around the corner. The victim
Watches the balanced ledger cancel out
And thinks of no more thinking. Clever death
Has done the brain-work, added all the sums,
And snapped the book together.
                              Well, old mind,

Are you free?

                Beyond desire and possibility.

How will you push up earth, then, strengthless one?

        My job is not to push; it is to see,
        And I see very well that what is done
        Is done, and all the fears flesh felt for me
        Break, weaker than the threads of Lilliput,
        Leaving me what I am.

Oh, speak to me
And tell me you are sorry for your strife.

        Sorry? Oh no. Mine was a merry life.
        Pain frightened me
        Until my own flesh felt it. Now I see
        That everything that I ever feared before
        Was hearsay, and each actual pain I bore
        Came in the purest spirit of comedy.

Variation on a Line From Shakespeare's Sixty-Fifth Sonnet

Watched and well known to the police, he walks
The Garden of the Oil Press. The great trees
Sweat in the mist, their moisture-swollen trunks
Flesh-like to touch. The cup
Of nausea for man, being filled up
And emptied now, he goes
To wake eleven sleepers
Lest they lack sight to see Iscariot close
As lithely as a springe for garroting sparrows.

This is the man. This is the arch-traitor
To land   bread   progress   family
Israel   Rome   and every other power
Whose action is stronger than a flower,

In time and just in time turning the minor
Star we live on like some great airliner
Back to the course direct, till every eye
Center by two crossed sticks stuck in a skull,
Between a criminal and a criminal,
The power
Whose action is no stronger than a flower.

Summer Unbound

The House on Pleasant Street

Nobody
Lived there in my time. The ground was full
Of granite outcroppings—and walking by
Alone in late November in the rain

You knew the tangled grass was all rock under.
Its wooden domes and cupolas had grown
Gray through and through, and there were several signs,
KEEP OFF, NO TRESPASSING, as gray as they,

But in the high top windows there was still
Glass to catch the sunsets. You might say,
"Someone is in. How soon their lights are on!"
Until you looked again. They pulled it down

Because it was too big for anyone,
And the employed built for the unemployed
A terraced park there. Lonely walkers now
No longer smell sweet-grass and mullein-weed

Rankling in the rain like an old wound
But sweet deodorant from the comfort station,
And caretakers complain
Of lovers and newspapers on the lawn.

Granite City

The granite sidewalks and the granite warrens
Of granite houses on the granite hills
Keep them warm enough, and roses, roses
Still in October, still now in November
Charge their back gardens, dooryards, window sills.

Every stoop is scrubbed to the mineral bone;
Every lamppost holds a basket up
For wastepaper and newspaper. Bars and such
Dissolute lackeys to dissolving nature
Lurk in back alleys, close at half past nine.

Calvin incarnated in granite here
What Euclid crystallized, and precious time
(Since every steeple has a clock in it)
And God are one, and man predestinate
To a good tombstone. Tombstones anyway

Are a flourishing local industry,
And many an aging Aberdonian
In Lima, Vladivostok, or Cape Town
Orders his tombstone here who does not know
How much rock is shipped from Norway now.

For the gleaming town between the Dee and the Don
Is running out of granite, but the year
She carves her final weapon in the war
Of wind and rain with memory, the rose
Will storm her steeples and be conqueror.

Londoners

hate the past. Only Americans
get excited about it. If you're strangled
with cold castles and monuments to the dead
good and bad clutter the public ways
and forms for filling fill your nights and days
you don't necessarily love them because they are there.

Still, there they are: you stand in a queue and stare
at miles of chimney pots and masonry
and say: I live here, I have lived here
in soot, chill, patience, and courtesy
and the cool of the Thames of a summer evening
eating a bun on a bench watching the shipping,

and glory too, of course, but glory has
gravity and does not move so fast
as citizens of the United States past
craters between building and building
and old solidities no longer there:
there are no bomb-holes in America.

Postwar Landscape

Insulate, unhyssoped, shy of song,
These strong and clever hands stretched out toward good
Weave Egypt over gardens
They will not see, they cannot seed. The world
Soots over; only barracks and airport
Shine clear, and in an hour
These, too, will all be sooted over. Only
The sky's delicate, soft-coal-smoke gray
Is real, and all production fawns on war.
Lear's little dogs, Tray, Blanche, and Sweetheart, see
How they bark! Who is the running man?
Allons enfants! the telescreen within
Instructs the children in the Master Plan.
And all who thought to find
Love in the waste of time between wars
Or clambering the mind's interstices
In catch-as-catch-can liberty, some wind
Frank, cold, blowing for unknown seas,
Gnaw the cotton bread of unison;
For when they are alone
The thundering engine of the mechanical heart
Laboring to lift the world above the world
By pure force, screams in their ears, and song
Ceases, or if it start
Hardens in the hardening of art.

Twinkling

Under the sullen of a Surrey fall
Let sun but for a moment well and spill
Out of the overcast, and every door
(How bright they paint their doors!) and every flower—
Wildflower, bush, and beech-leaf suddenly are
Wild with the colors of Jerusalem.

John's Vision, quick as a cat's claw
Snatches you in, and there
Shining with every gem and precious stone
Stands the Indelible City Blake saw
In the pulsation of an artery
And in another, gone.

Hometown

Malden, city of my dead youth,
City of tired sleepers and no glories,
Detoured by Paul Revere, where Sacco's ghost
Wails round the Baptist church; city of Judson,
Bringer of light to Burma, who dying there
Never knew how dark it grew elsewhere;

City of Sunday mornings deep with bells
Where under elms and maples with my father
I walked to a church that smelt of damp plaster
(I thought it then the smell of rectitude)
And one day heard my pretty Sunday School teacher
Tell how they crucified Christ and when I cried
Somebody kicked me hard under the table.

City of Cross Street, city of Suffolk Square,
The ghetto where an older man I knew
Bought pumpernickel — he was a Christian, too—
And jam and cream cheese, and traded with a Jew
Because he liked the man. The neighbors said
He read too much and wasn't all there,

But when the fog rolled up from the Lynn Marsh
And Linden and Revere and we went in,
Beside the Mystic River he had seen
A vision of our City where the sun
Of Campanella, Booker Washington,
Veblen, and Lincoln Steffens, and Einstein
Shines equally on every honest man.

Occupied Territory

We are not the first
Inhabitants, the sole proprietors,
Nor thrid the mazes of the Minotaur

With lucky string. Nature is innocent
Of nothing, nothing. Only a tissue thin
Curtain in the brain shuts out the coiled

Recumbent Landlord. Lift it and look there,
There where among huge alien stones the hawk
Leans to the singular scream of the struck hare.

Apparition

Sun, moon, and stars forever stalking me,
Give me a sense of nakedness. It is
Hard for one so much in the public eye
To be perfectly natural. Nevertheless,
As I strolled out this evening minding my business

And trying to put the best possible face on things,
My stick (I am, unfortunately, blind)
Encountered this resilient projection.
I poked again, and then, the wind veering,
Gave up a most unpleasant exhalation.

The odor would have turned me, but the corpse,
Shuddering, trembling, stirring,
Screamed in the shattering
Way they have: "Away! Get away! Leave me
To contemplate the facts of my condition

Without your apparition. Of all things,
What starts my eyes and freezes up my marrow
Most is blind, bodiless, gray
Specters like you!" With an apology,
I backed away. How shall we love each other,

When, as they say in volumes on theology,
We embrace on Resurrection Day?

Tapestry

For Myra Mayo

Lady, my love and all my sole desire,
Ruling our harsh antagonist, Rumor's
Ugly tongues, with the strong skill you have,
Love and sustainer of the triple loves
That love us and are loved more than the tongue's
Power to utter — caught in a mystery
That weaves their little loves through iron wires

That spring may leap magnanimous with flowers
Beyond the tongues of prophecy, and grass
Softer than eyelashes of head-on-arm
Children asleep from play. The Unicorn's
Flickering silver lightning and the roar
Of my Gold Lion guard your garden, Lady.
Oh all my senses are

Yours, smell, touch, taste, see, hear what I may
And in your rich pavilion, jewelry
Rarer than all the gems of India spreads
Astonishment. That you weave this for me
Puzzles the world, but the Artificer
Who weaves the world, from his high Judgment Seat
Where tongue, eye fail, commends your tapestry.

To a Friend Teaching
in the Provinces

For John Doyle

As you say, John, it is narrowing
And cold, and if the soul was ever sublime
It has forgotten where and what it was,
"Peace" rhymes with "cease." Was there another rhyme?

Bombs help, but we never needed them to tell
What we have learned of apples above all:
Gravitation made the apple fall
With the connivance of a certain worm

That nibbled Newton too, and nibbles
Us and our green ball till every star
Slips like popcorn to explosion.
Therefore we fight. This is the true war

Fought in the narrow skull's, the heavy heart's
Remotest provinces, and we are sent
Against the universal coils with fire
To light the dull, warm the intelligent.

The Return of Prospero

Prospero, bury that big book
Fifty fathom deep, and turn, turn
Back to Milan: responsibility
Up to the waist, up to the lips again.

They nudge each other, say Look, Look,
His beard is hawthorne and his crown is gold,
And you possess the world
In double sovereignty having the popular will.

But Ariel, the adorable potentate
Who whipped waves wild or made them rear
Back on themselves and sleep, is ransomed now
And Caliban raised to a million

Your proper study. Magic was a kind
Of politics but less empirical,
For things above have their equation
In things below, as water, fire, and air;

But since the Demon fouled
Sycorax, man is ruled by man—
Even by the True Prince, even in Milan—
Somewhere between despair and miracle.

Letter to Too Many People

Now—as if it mattered: there are so many people
    writing so many poems—I write to you
To say that everyone is still
    very well, although
Somewhat beside themselves, there being more to do
    than they can do, and airplane pilots higher
    up in the air than we are
    look freer.
Feet, feet, feet, feet, feet
For all their being cocked up in evening's seat
    are never quite rested by morning any more,
    and hair
    grows rare.
Friends that I miss,
I think there's something specious in all this.
And so I set my face
    rigidly (but secretly of course)
    against the whole elaborate apparatus
    designed, or so I guess, from the very first
    simply to wear us out.
"The more angels the more room," said Swedenborg
    and the machines
    in rubber factories that wear out tires
    almost instantaneously say the same thing
    and all our bonfires
    of sugar, coffee, potatoes, human beings
    so bright they can be seen in Asia
    with peculiar distinctness.
Too many people see by these contents
    the American way
    of living graciously.
It is very simple what these people see;
But not knowing which were the greater courtesy,
to tell truth or make you a little happier,
I mutter beside myself uncertainly

as a bull in a china shop, a lion among ladies,
    a monkeywrench
    or, as the English say,
    more elegantly, a spanner
in man's most delicate machinery:
    honesty in a letter.

Homage to Vincent

Pass, painter of proud Europe's summer, down
Mind-twisted ways to Torquemada-brown
Hecatombs of leaves and summer's end.
Let grass and clover intermixed with weeds
Incise, and the deft, delicate roots of trees

Gather up your wound. The flickering hordes
Of blackbirds that attacked your ripened grain
And all those insupportable evergreens
That whispered at your back have their reward:
The yoke is lifted from your neckbone.

And that proud Europe that possessed your ear
Slumbers in sorrow on her bloody arm.
Over the puddles of her abattoir
The lean days draw immitigably down,
But on her fortresses and cold cafés

Your stars, enormous and compassionate,
Like sunflowers still undiminished shine;
And in her glory's late
Babylonian captivity
Your lunacy alone ordered her mind.

The Sleeping Beauty

In a place where hunchbacks and old women
Quarreled in their thin voices all the day
This temporizing grew intolerable:
I knew that here the Sleeping Beauty lay.

(Had they known it all the time and been
Sly servitors where I could only seize
Bad temper and distorted images?)
Sight ended the old argument. I saw

Her tower clear against the star-picked blue
Over their hovels. It was no affair
Of a cloud and the moon's subtle conjunction; thorns
Hatched me all criss-cross as I hacked my way through

And stumbled bloody still and breathing still
Into a country where no footsteps fall
And where from moat, to keep, to citadel
Spider-webs lie like water.

I silvered as I entered through the door
Where time cannot prevail
But howls outside forever where I found her
Asleep, beautiful, the cobwebs round her.

Poem for Gerard

Understand too late? Of course we can:
The love of everything, like winnowing,
Scatters the spirit like fine dust, plum-bloom
Over the world. Heart must be held, held down
Of its own will, chained, hooded and become
Deaf to itself and dumb

To hear things speak themselves in their sole tongue.
By stress and instress are their songs wrung
Out of them, scaped and bruited; to possess
Their breathing outwardness the eye must go
In to their root and onward to their end
Perishing with their vanishing to span

From germ to the full grain
Mountain or martyr, chestnut-leaf or man.
It makes the blood run cold, warm flesh glower
To think of you, Windhover,
Cleaving so bleak a wind, maneuvering
Sight more than any in how sealed an hour.

The Prince of Odd
and Anger

For Dylan Thomas

The Prince of Odd and Anger,
The Contrary King's son—
No foster child I sing—
Could do anything
Except betray the lust
Overreaching dust
And the laconic worm
To raise up to the sun
Incorruptible rhyme.

Our wooden leg of words
Sprouts his green leaf sadly
That burgeoned and skipped gladly
Under his regimen.
Whatever *we* had done,
The sooner if done badly,
If better done, yet soon
He took a counter-path
Into the sullen wood.

Now in multitude
We revel in a garden
Eye had never seen
In all Arden
When winds are in the North
But for his setting forth.

To the Archpoet

On bulls, and wearing roses,
The men with varnished faces,
The boys who never were young
Stripped for the tired town.

"But you," the nightwind said,
"Be night; pretend you're dead;
Yet listen, shivering, chill,
For April and her bird.

"Despair, Despair, Despair
Nibbles flake by flake
That dainty carrousel
Art for Art's Sake. Go wear

"Sackcloth beneath your neat
Business suit; go eat
Hunger for your meat
With the most elegant air.

"Let the mad old, the dead young
Behave their have, but you,
Attentive to the throe
Of the nightwind, O

"Archpoet and polymath,
Become what you have heard:
A mouth without a tongue
Singing contrition in

"A world without a word."

Letter to My Grandfather's Picture

When you were a boy, Grandfather, you lived on a farm
Sturdily, and, as soon as you could,
Homesteaded, and had a farm of your own.
But slavery? You chose the Cavalry
(You spelt it "Calvary"), one leg for two,
The City, and a little jewelry store;
The factory at last. You died of a stroke
Down at the Mill, fixing the factory clock,

And fixed it very well. That Mill
Has knitted now till every boy and girl
Enters it as the world. The spindles
Carry the yarn in zigzags and tilted angles
Which enters every color under heaven
And leaves but one. You took your time a little
In your day, Grandfather, but now the whistle
Whistles Sundays, holidays, and all.

You wouldn't pray, they say, after the war
But read *The Law of Psychic Phenomena*
Hoping perhaps—being a watchmaker—
To find whatever mainspring made things go.
Then the clock struck. As you climbed up the ladder
Viewing the loom's perspective altogether,
Did all that speeding yarn outline a figure,
A hanging figure, hanging in pain? or can

This be glimpsed only from flat on the floor?
And is it finished on some other floor?
We never see the thing we have worked on
Whirling from revolution to revolution
Through the Mill's long explosion.
Yet do not lean out of the picture, Grandfather;
Though you cried out like Jesus and Jehovah
I could not hear you through the spindles' roar.

The Monitor Reports

The man who will cut his throat, and the man who will twist
From some high office-building window kissed
The girl who will end in a gas oven one of these days.
The bartender, who will die of psittacosis
At the age of 80, served them with Four Roses
Knowing better than they do what it is.

Then there entered in the sad young man
In a gray overcoat who does not know
That every living room and every bar
In all the world contains a time machine.
He was timidly smiling. Every customer
Eyed him with horror, shuddered to recognize

Such ignorance of the future in a face:
It was an insult to the human race
To contemplate the withering-away
With eyes so hideous with hope—as if
All were not finished to the end of time
To the last foreseen eyelash, charted breath.

Then Razor-throat, reacting sharply, said:
"Slice me in segments!" The Jumper only snored:
"Drop dead!" into his seventh glass.
Only the fair asphyxiate to be,
Into her monitored, unprivate wire,
Promptly reported the anomaly,

Saying: "It is a breach of our known fate,
Your guaranty of withering-away
Which is our peace. How can we sleep at night
Dogged by the Unstatistical Man? To me
(These were her actual words in black and white)
It smacks of outright immortality."

The Gentle People

The Gentle People said, "We've too much power
Of traction for an overt act of war,"
And drew together in a bomb-shelter
To hobble violent Nature and become
Still in the heart of Pandemonium.

They voted to become invisible
And wear a gray, impenetrable caul
Over their faces while their shoulders
Propped the heavy hills, the hanging hours
That hid their Occupation from our eyes

Protestant within, unreconciled
To what the Eye sees upon this star
That the Heart cannot know, they stilled and still
Likerous tides in the full moon. I fear
The world revolves more slowly every year.

We shall not feel the weapon in the hands
The Gentle People lay upon our lands
Till pitchers broken at the cistern fill
With fullness over, the Daughters of Music sing,
There is no more sea, the sun stands still.

The Gracious Ones

The poor things wear
Thin, and very often I suppose
Grow very hungry. It's hard in the sun's glare
(And neon's glare) to fear the Gracious Ones.
Living and dying
More brilliantly than moths or butterflies
Or those small, moving, asymmetrical
Lights called stars that fade out every morning,
We fly and burn, and only
Science fiction or a murder tale
Makes us wonder, *Are they faithful?*

Even our well-mannered children
Are noisier, more fractious far than these,
And when they sleep and give us a moment's peace,
Before we look, before we realize,
The heavy lids of our eyes
Fall, cover us. Come now, Gracious Ones,
Now while the still finger-propped avalanche
Hangs suspended, seize
This passing hour to harrow and accuse.
Censure us as you please.

As to this rumor of a victory, none
Really believe the King will ever return;
And if at last, swollen with plunder,
He should come home, naturally we
Must do what seems best for the family.
What crime is it, and what
Expiation falls, what proper doom
On folks who have but tried to set in order
And make a house a home?

Such is our story. Every citizen
Will witness us in this. Are you deaf? dumb?

Furies? or out walking? or asleep?
Walk softly, then, and if you slumber, breathe
Quietly and do not let your drone
Penetrate the painted nursery door
Where Electra clasps her teddy-bear,
And small Orestes, the day's battle won,
Sleeps with dead soldiers and a plastic gun.

Ptyx

Sur les crédences, au salon vide: nul Ptyx,
Aboli bibelot d'inanité sonore
(Car le maître est allé puiser des pleurs au Styx
Avec ce seul objet dont le Néant s'honore).
—Mallarmé

"Hold this!" I held it. We were outside Time
In the cold and the dark and trying to get in.
Just then something gave, and there I was
In broad daylight holding this instrument.
You were cavorting all over the meadow
In hot, strong sun. I called but you were gone
Across the brook, beyond the apple trees
Where I could just make out the smoke of chimneys.

Now the trinket that I held in my hand
Was obsolete, a thing of empty sound,
A worn and dusty Ptyx; yet this alone
Had sprung the barrier and throbbing screen
That on this side seems but a manhole cover,
But under, all the difference between
Time and not-Time. I stood there missing you
More than the morning light could understand.

For you had sloughed me and the Ptyx too
For spaciousness and the world's multitude,
Not doubting for a moment that all good,
Naked, and all real, waited in Time
Where now you hunted it. The gold sun
Shone on the Ptyx, and as I held it there
With summer a foregone conclusion
The whole green meadow called it sinister.

For "Who," said buttercup and timothy,
And "Who," the tree toads in strict antiphon,
And "Who," the rich rocks and established trees,

"Would make a mock of such an afternoon
Or pry beyond it to the crack of doom?"
I knew, but held my tongue thinking of your
Odyssey of admiration
And the rich circle of your willed return.

So I held the Ptyx till rock shadows
Stretched like elastic and the last apple
Hanging unpicked, pecked at by birds, fell
And plashed to cider under the feet of cattle,
Till Fall's far-flung auroral rhetoric
Faded and set, the black cat got my tongue,
And in the gunny-sack of the world's night
The Great Bear, all seven stars blazing, hung

And hangs gazing over my left shoulder.
Always I clutch the Ptyx, contented now
To gather in it a few Stygian tears.
(They polarize on earth.) Nothing's sole honor,
The Ptyx, alone considers what it is
Ice cannot find, alone can spring the cover
That closes all. The hunt is over: Hunter
Who once at dayspring cried "Hold this," *hold this.*

The Coming of the Toads

"The very rich are not like you and me,"
Sad Fitzgerald said, who could not guess
The coming of the vast and gleaming toads
With precious heads which, at a button's press,
The flick of a switch, hop only to convey
To you and me and even the very rich
The perfect jewel of equality.

Making Your Poem

Begin it only if you must. At first
You'll surely miss the poem at which you aim,
Then hit it perfectly some other time
When you are aiming elsewhere. You will find
Everything coming out quite different.
To your astonishment the reader's mind
Will change it imperceptibly, and then
The poem itself will seem to you to disdain
You and your sweating thought—it's a wise poem
Knows its own father. I've had one
Cut me dead in the street. A poem solves
Only itself, serves but itself, and he
Who makes one can never go back again
To what he was, nor yet be poetry.

One

The unstable lights in the sky, the unaccountable
Behavior of dials and all clocks proclaim
Time's end—and no one is responsible.
With many a chipped chime and cracked gong
Towers toll the end of balancing
Power against power, and arranging
Cleverly, with the utmost energy,
The matter of our last humiliation.

No one is responsible. All, all
Have excellent reasons. Has no Irishman
In the blind language of the setting sun
Told its coming on? Have no wise men
Patiently following a wizened star
Through the all-seeing Eye on Palomar
Reported in the patined sky no pattern
But the pattern of Process unwinding a snapped spring?

No. It is certain the slow dust will fur
Man, his machine; mouse, his breadcrumb
And in these sleeping streets no flickering
Telescreen or cry of baby can
Waken the world unless the brazen bird
Called Chanticleer, in perfect doom's domain,
Crow in the grasp of his delusion
Crow to bring up the sun till one man
Waken, and weep, and hear the clocks strike ONE.

The Myth and the Makers

Pomp, circumstances, varying lords, or a lass
Run every world-Atlas
On his own sword in the end, where, unlike Charles,
It never occurs to him to apologize
For his unconscionable time a-dying.
The purple slowly pumping out of him,
An Antony for pure amazement cries,
"I'm dying, Egypt, dying!"

No god, no god; and yet the tawny queen
Who taught her weeping to the crocodile
Found sweet the venom of a mothered worm
For lack of him. Because an Antony
Dies as he has lived, largely;
Empires crumble where his knees give way,
Chasm where he hits, and all his loves
Buckle in landslides to his open grave.

What is this "greatness" that a change in the wind,
The fluctuation of a lady's mind
Should shuck the world, and mere Ability
With a head for double-entry bookkeeping
Re-possess, re-finish, put it on?
Look about you at their sufferings then
And hear poor Tom and Nan wearily pray:
Good Lord deliver us from Great Men.

Yet in a month ploughed under Antony
Stumbles in vulgar verse; the balladeers
Heave him aloft on Fortune's Ferris Wheel;
Shoe-clerks ponder him between pay days.
Wherever Hope turns in a hopeless maze
Antony stirs. First the green blade
That looks like grain, and then the ear of steel,
And then the harvest, red, corruptible

And all is as it was. Who builds these tall
Myths-in-the-flesh, omniresponsible
To myth as to their millions millionaires?
What are their names to whom all in the world
Not noble to the bone, purple in grain
Is fiat paper, pious fraud, and weighs
Less than a feather on the scale of days
Against one careless shrug of Antony's?

They are cold Tom and hungry Nan
Who on this world's flat screen
Project in shining fourth dimension
Fate cannot reach or bend, an Antony
Scattering kings like nickels from his hands
And, fishing off the docks with him, his Queen
To light through coughs, bad air, gum wrappers thrown,
Their trudge through the alone to the alone.

The Ringing

In your hand; it is within your hand
And therefore inaccessible and you
Also walk the Valley of Desolation
Among the thousand thousands.

It is more
Than flesh can bear; it breaks under it; therefore
So many and so many in the night
Dream their tomb, assuming in the dream
The prenatal posture.

There was a teacher
Once who in a blackboard found a door
Into a garden, into a green garden,
And everyone who wished could enter there.
Then the bell rang.

It is still ringing.
The patient, tolerant substance
Of which we make our tables and our chairs
Has not heard it and is in the garden
Through our conversation,

And through
Our longest wars steel itself is still.
Bird, insect, dog, everything animal
Knows this, and if they look at us at all
Look sadly at us

Over the warm wall—
Excluded not by pang or any pain
(They pay as gladly for the beautiful
As we do), but this endlessly clanging bell.

The Dial and the Mole

In Memoriam: Simone Weil, 1909-1943

> What the common basis was, both at home
> and abroad is not easy to define. In those
> days it was unnecessary to formulate it; at
> the present time it becomes impossible to
> formulate.
>
> —T. S. Eliot in *The Unity of*
> *European Culture*

Quite casually we nodded, shared in talk
Whatever occurred to us, and still the lull
Grew like a bubble till it held all:
Your house, my house; your children on this lawn,
Mine on the other lawn, and in between
As far as we could see there was no line,
Picket, or privet-hedge, or wire wall—
Only this common sundial where you
Sometimes told the time and I too
Divided us. There was no other world.

Then, overnight, all split; each hemisphere
Shut sharply in the better to exclude
All but one view: its own. In every skull
The fissure deepened, yawned interminable,
And every loyal citizen thriftily shored
His neighbor's ruins. Only a little mole
That crept unnoticed under either wall
Too late to matter, treasonous to mind,
As winter deepened the dividing line
Lived in the country of the sundial.

The Poet
Who Talks to Himself

The poet who talks to himself
In despair
Or to an audience of
Air,

Married to the poem,
Knows once for all
What nagging lies between
The *will* and the *shall*;

Perceives that beauty is not
Thought, but the object of thought
And dances to its end
Hovering in the wind

Like doves, to settle down
About some casual man
Offering a casual crumb
Or not, as casual can,

Both being portion of
The carelessness of love
Which finds the perfect rhyme
Nowhere and in no time.

The Match

'Tis Might, half slumbering on
its own right arm
—John Keats

Put sinew in it, for it never was
chined prose—that
smells of phosphorescent fat. Your poet
knows sensation and the mind's play
are not the lot: only the only way
to rule all things together, rein and ride
once more over the scared, indignant town
the courser of Medusa's founted blood
and Death's astonishment. With words, then,
common as dirt, but soundly skeletoned
as a good house, resilient as grain
make it if you can; and when your door
thunders and it is Time, invite Time in
and let them try which is the mightier,
he or this Babe who chokes in either hand
a dead serpent that did not understand.

The Shapers

Troglodytes, stretched in their cobalt cave,
The clouds loll, lulled by the thrilling music
And lightning logarithms of the wind.

Rapscallions, they loll and do not care
What their wheeling shadows do down here
Engulfing or releasing. A moment ago

I was swallowed by a cloud shadow,
Who now sit blinking here in the sun's glare.
The wind's invisible; and yet the wind

Shapes processions of fortuitous cloud
As fortune shapes the mind, or as the tongue
The flux of words that rises from the brain

Shapeless and without form, so I command
And canvas a tall ship to sail the sea.
Its masts break into leaves; its leaves flower

Into a city, tower on white tower
That would last forever, but the wind
Writhes under my hand; and as stone walls

Alter in spring when the frost melts and thaws,
All comes down. As the wind does to clouds,
The clouds to us, we do

Not as boys drown a miserable kitten
But to reshape anew
All images until they correspond

To the face and image of one man
We know and do not know
Before we pass under the next shadow.

164

Do Not Feed the Elephant

O closed in glass, clothed in impenetrable
Crystal, walk among us, gracious
Ice among fever, fresh air among gas,
But whether with peanuts or with *aequitas*

Do not feed the elephant. It is
What it is—a trunk, a leaf, a wall,
A tongueless snake, or two sharp scimitars—
The doctors differ—you alone are free
To watch in silence and be wonderful.

Wound in our webs of wisdom, we can see
Better than you our rich, our eloquent
Subjectivity, but you are sent
That we may freely know our punishment:

Kindly do not feed the elephant.

Spring Is Coming

They say the blood of winter, color of rye,
Shall yet unclot and flow in the street of spring.
Let the king do as he pleases, live delicately;
Time is *his* king.

But I must get on with my work, consume,
This heap of paper on the office table
Steadily, gradually. The room
Is austere and bare, a scholar's room

So let the man knock. I have no lack;
Why should I let him in?
But I can't keep my mind on my work, am not myself
In this uproar.

(All within of course, in the nerves, in the mind.
The king, they say, is half dead, half blind
With the same sound.) Perhaps the visitor
Has friends behind him, and they, friends, and they, friends.

But if I opened the door and the king himself
Flopped forward onto the floor for the spring to breed
Maggots in, weedwheels, wildflowers,
I should go out of my mind,

For terror's phthisic crystal
Cracking all over town with the king's death
Avalanches would roar from a thousand houses,
And I never should get these papers corrected.

Swim

The first thing you saw was a man.
He stood on the bank making geometrical figures.
As fast as his finger traced them on the air
The glittering ovals, rhomboids, circles fell
Into the stream and were carried away. The stream
Consisted entirely of them.
And if a few were more opaque than others,
None were so black you could not see the brown
Earth-bed through their swift procession.

You thought yourself quite different at the time,
But looking at involves, and once in
You were carried away. What had seemed mere diagram
Floating about at various distances
Resolved itself while moving side by side
At incredible speed to children, women, men.
You touch, as though at rest, again and again,
And think, "They are a part of me," and dream,
"They are more truly me than I am."

Yet you remember the great artisan
Who never ceased from labor, and know further
You can emerge from the stream at any time
To watch his work. Perhaps it would be better
(Trying is the best philosopher)
To stand on the bank and swim below in the stream
At one and the same time. But having grown
Accustomed to the medium of water
Everything outside appears disorder.

Yet once you did, and therefore must again
Lift a foot, a knee, an eye, a hand
Wholly outside the element and climb
The highest bank to view the waters of
Your last immersion. And as the first

Plunge into water chilled you to the bone,
So on the sand in naked air you'll drown
Until you draw the first deep lungful in.
Air is a thing too clear to be made plain;

Blake's way was to say quite simply:
I bound Time to my left foot like a bright sandal
To walk forward through Eternity.
But could he take it off when he put it on?
Departure is return. The smoky dawn
Will be early still, the maker making,
When you break surface and rear up there,
One foot on the bank, one foot still in,
Knowing your nature is amphibian.

Summer Unbound

A leaf fell just now,
Bronze as an Indian squaw,
Warm and dead, indubitably so,
Twirling in my office window
It settled on my typewriter, and I

Let it lie. Why should I tap on
Through Indian Summer's satisfaction
With itself, and who am I to disturb
Death's ideal working conditions? Lie
Still, brown leaf. But I,

Closing the door, must carry my conclusions
Past ART and ECONOMICS through the warm
Campus where above me a jet plane
Like a surrealist poet whose metaphor
Exceeds his grasp, outstripping its own rasp,

Inscribes a line tinged by the sinking sun
On the high, blue, Babylonian wall.
I too might crisp and fall
If I could read that bright inscription.
It may be Shelley's friend,

Again unbound, scoops more
Of the essential flame than heretofore
And crammed
With pure philanthropy and hydrogen
Dives back towards earth to give it all to men.

Handbag

For generations mothers, daughters, grandmothers
Have carried one. Curiously fine
The click it makes, separating time
Past from time present with
Matter-of-factness, tangibility.

When you snapped yours just then, suddenly
I could not think woman grows wholly woman
Until she has one. It has the sound
Of a mind made up before the mind
Knows what it has done. White-armed

Helen must have lifted one just so
And clicked it so when the gray Argive sand
First felt the keel of the black ship from Troy—
And in that moment had already come,
A tall white flame, to kindle Ilium.

The Swimmers

Under the sea was our equation:
Language slid from us and our fluid eyes
Welled comfort and despair; under this world
Our crystal and invisible angels
Not without blood altered their idiom.

Dry is the shore, and the sun's paradigm
Declines all shell to shale; inflected fin
Crisps to a curl, drops off, and gill is gone.
Moist, sullen creatures under a damp stone
Slink from the sun's abstraction, but we

Poised on a forked, laborious stratagem,
Plunge inland willy-nilly, far from home,
Engrossing air, swallowing sun, but our
Ensutured caves contain the ocean still:
In every hollow shell we lift to ear

The combers roar, and as we walk the gray
Endlessly hurrying multitude of sand
Equal, particular, and uniform,
The sea surrounds our bones' transition;
As we pass through the desert yet we swim.

Fall Abstract

Autumn was quick this year: the squirrels worked
Harder for acorns; almost everywhere
I saw the scuttle of a furry nation
With button eyes on a foregone conclusion

I cannot see; and all I know is when
My vacuum cleaner with a sudden spurt
Gobbled some tacks the children had left on the floor
I heard machine-gun fire and hit the dirt.

Tonight I saw the moon
Stick in the crotch of the oak outside my house—
But not for long, as I moved it came loose.
Whichever way I turn, wherever I look

Everything seems immortal but the soul
And these oakleaves. I watch them as they fall,
Noting in ugly abstract symbols how
They hightail down at the first touch of frost

(Yet some that rattle like sore throats will cling),
And sometimes when a raker bending down
Kindles them, the coughing and the tears
Sprung from a single, simple seed of flame.

Deity

"When I go back . . . "; but the rockfall
Spoiled all that, the air unbreathable
And the tunnel crammed, stuffed with so much
Indubitably rich rubbish, rubbish still
All but impenetrable. But yet note down, Pencil
Of light I write by, neither weak nor strong
But narrowly sufficient, having paused
Long enough by this low wall to see:
That every moment bears the next moment
Out of a womb that snaps like a trap, as hard
As the adamant around us and that God
Is dead in history (perfect) and daily dies
More minutely in all backward eyes;
That only at this end of the passage is
(The wombs being closed that bore us) Deity.

The Loss

If I much concern myself with this,
You do too, and all who do not seem
Stone faces dreaming stone's dream
Of nothing, nothing, like the images
On Easter Island. All the animals
Follow us with their eyes as we go by
Wondering what we look for. In the sky
Red fades out to black and the night falls,
Night and the ignorance of eyes; but we
Light matches, matches; on our hands and knees
Ransacking every hummock, every tree's
Droppings for any nickel, dime, or cent
Of the incredible emolument
We never lost until we looked to see.

Three Ladies

My first is rare and gracious, courtesy
And light and darkness mingle in her face:
She dwells at day's end in a most luminous place:
Food, wine, and lanterns of civility.

My second scorns such gross and bodily
Clinging to houses and rich provender,
Saying it ripens like a yellow pear
Only for others, rots for itself; and she

(My second lady) hunts a dangerous prey
Through harsh, unsettled pastures where burdock
Sticks to her clothes but cannot bar her way
And eats wild grapes, a native of the rock.

My third, in blue, sits on a stone nearby
A little covered basket. The babe in her lap
Lifts in his fists a bunch of grapes which she
Plucks as she will and feeds him grape by grape.

None are for her. Her husband for their fare
Hurls his long staff up into a nut tree
To knock a handful down. The donkey there
Stares at the infant lovingly, sadly.

My first is rich; my second, fleet of foot,
Outstrips the world; my third pities its care.
And all the three are one; the one is three.
There are no other ladies anywhere.

Praise for the Earthkeepers

Earthkeepers, how agile are your ways,
Your strategies still able to elude
The claws of the mountains that close over us.

All your hot heroes who attempt those tors
And come back shivering, blubbering blood, to say
"That way's impassable! Don't try that way!"

Would never have tried in the first place at all
Did you not know your course
Right from the moment of their setting forth:

And through the longest night, the shortest day
Trim, fill, and set ablaze
Every lamp you have, for thus they,

Teetering destruction by destruction,
Recall the earthkeepers and in the daze
And light of light beyond all light turn,

Cacodemon winds, down, down,
Toward your spark upon the breathable floor
And the doomed valley they have whistled for.

Moving

Moving from one poised intelligibility
To another, out of life, out of time,
How anxiously, looking before, behind,
Above, below, we leave the lumpedness,
Substance without form, the Devil's heart
Extended endlessly in pure duree,
The horrible concreteness of living;

The furtive way thoughts creep up from behind
And pounce on us! the beautiful, if true
A panther met, a flicker passing and
Hurting with its blessing. Ugliness,
The shadow cast by all we are and do,
Slinks through the vegetation. Only abstraction,
The swift malevolent whiteness Ahab knew

In bank, bench, legislature, laboratory
Lures us at last, for it is blind as a bat
To flesh and blood, but as old Chekhov said
When someone asked him if he liked the sea:
"Yes. Only it's so empty,"
And stepping poised, stepping delicately,
Added, "The sea is difficult to describe."

Snow Scene

This is a snow scene on rice paper. (I
Forget the artist's name.) The feathery
Flakes are falling still, and someone
Wearing a snow-peaked coolie-hat shoulders
A snowy burden, and his old horse too

Carries a load that comes to a peak of snow.
Both move toward a village in the pines.
Whether the man who leads the horse is you,
Or whether on immaculate rice paper
In Japan three hundred years ago

You saw it and your brush defined the scene,
You too set black on white, or reading lines
Black on white, shoulder, in an expanse
As innocent as this
A burden that grows always heavier

As you advance
With this piled whiteness, which,
When you look closer
Turns out to be the ground of the whole picture,
Nothing, the clean rice paper showing through.

Joy of Man's Desiring

Needle sliding in the groove,
Resurrect undying love:
Shining metal, turn again—
Past the whisper in the brain
Of its own destruction—
Thought to intuition:

You have reason, Reason none,
For it filters coldly down
Towers black with soot this light
That is neither day nor night
But darkness rational, late star
Of him who shall be Lucifer

Nevermore, and underground,
Mathematically bound,
Fractions all till nova brim
White light over Bethlehem.
Still emerge from the machine
Light that Satan has not seen

On land or sea; and needle prove
Time's resistance until Love,
Born again in the dull cave
Of man's imagination, prove
Fidelity in more than wiring,
Jesu, joy of man's desiring.

Later Appearances

On the Third Tower

I found my freedom academic: on
The one hand The Tower of London stood,
And leaning gently over on the other
The Tower of Pisa; and their demonstration
Of gyves and odd weights falling equally
Carried conviction of Necessity.

Then what am I doing here?
What business have I on the Third Tower?
I don't recall clambering some back stair
Or being hoist by creaking windlass
Up this pharos, no philosopher
Reasoned me into it. I crouch here

Sparrow-small, cuffed at by wind, where cold
Punctilious stars patrol
Nightly, dull gulls by day.
The Tower shakes ceaselessly, and now again
The Old Man, flourishing his trident, howls
To the populous waves, his children:

Topple it once for all! O vertigo
And gap in nature, Freedom, I have come
To your Third Tower, revolving in my mind
The only beam of light that sailors find
On this bleak coast where spontaneity
Grinds in the last compulsion of the sea.

Query

I died and three lemons
Arranged asymmetrically
Took my place. Just why
Did you select that moment to comment on
The sweetness of my disposition?

Soon Now

Soon now snow will blow
Dark in the gray, yet white
Seen on coatsleeve or hat
It will accumulate
Stealthily and yet
In twenty minutes or less
You would not know the place.
It will hiss and race
Blanket and swath and shroud
All spring and summer bred
And autumn disavowed;
All things are allowed
Just so it carapace
What would not look ahead
Prefering the old ways.
For sleepers under it
It weaves a warm, dark wool;
For all who walk abroad
Dazzled in morning light
Whiteness, white, white, white.

184

Crossing

> The waters indeed are to the palate bitter
> and to the stomach cold.
> —Pilgrim's Progress

The first step in your instep turns to stone
Prod with the staff of your mind as far as you can,
The stream is murky. Transportation
Has improved but little on this river
Since Enoch and Elijah
Crossed it alive in fire. Under the stars'
Studied indifference to the blood's affairs,
You cross as heretofore.
                    The second step
Shudders to memory; you recollect
How stubbornly the dead hug what they have
And never yet
Hovered to convoy traveller, or set
His slipping foot sure on the farther shore.
It will seem to you the dead remember
Nothing, or too much.
                    No one
Who had not crossed here many times before
Under the crux of breath
And nailed to sense as I am and you are
In each particular
Could tell us where to put our third footstep;
Yet, saving this, a man might spend forever
Treading the bitter waters of no death.

What Shall I Say of You

For Robert Frost

What shall I say of you, my window-tree,
You have not said before, and better at that?
Only that I've watched your silhouette
Against the night and the Cartwright house next door

Gently decide; that I have seen you freeze
Patiently and breathing deep withdraw
Inside the hieroglyph and metaphor
Of your tough skeleton, and standing still

In glare ice still outlast
The last leaf and the grass,
Emerson and Whitman, winter's worst,
And rise your own green justification

With multitudinous tongue serenely talking
Whether or not we catch your drift until,
Like the blind man's, our eyelids lift
On men as trees, but walking.

The End of Prophecy

Brute sleep and pig soldiers
Eat our satisfaction. It is
Stultifying how this menopause
In God's wrath vanishes vision
Clamps and seals over like a manhole cover
Clean-flaming prophecy. The filthy shore
That we had sworn would soon
Swiftly and crisply be attended to
Harbours us now. And though perception
Tells us but little and that half in error,
We seem to meet the same smile over and over,
Flaccid and fat. It is infuriating
To feel complacence like a wall of wool
Fleecing our eyeballs of their pasture
Of all-consuming fire. Better to roll
In the black belly of the whale, be shot
Homeless and bare on some forbidding shore.
But no, the Lord God,
Who smote us till we did the thing he would,
And told us what to say,
Has ransomed every soul in Nineveh.
Even the green, green gourd
He whispered up to hood us from the heat
When we were tired out with saying sooth
Withers, and we had said
Blasphemy but that we overheard
Him talking to Himself in thunder
(Distantly, so as not to be understood):
Men, women, and cattle of Nineveh,
Behold my prophets. They are much put out
Hell treads not on the heel of prophecy.
Yet in your town stone would not stand on stone
Had you not heard and done
At least a modicum of what they said.
Now they were better dead

Until they see the end of prophecy
Always was and always will be
Non-fulfillment. Though the fire foretold
Sometimes falls, sometimes in spite of all
It need not and my prophets bring to pass
A future better than God knows it was.

When I Saw the Door

When I saw the door
Neither open nor shut
Neither locked nor unlocked,
That vast Head whose eyes
Are forever looked
Into me and I saw

Whether I run in fur,
Wat, the hunted hare,
Or pursue his track
And bell him till he dies
I move everywhere
Centered in those eyes.

Landscape

for Karl Mattern

Mattern's picture, Myra,
The one we saw at the one-man exhibition
Three years ago, remember?
Remember how it looked like heaped-on-canvas
Paint piled anywhere when we were going the rounds,

But when we were half way
Out of the gallery,
Glancing back casually,
We looked into an endless garden, a world
Depth beyond depth white, crimson, green, green-gold
And sun-gold everywhere,

A world we know is there
Because the enduring painter
Wielding his brushes as a crab its claws
Clipped and hung on to it though light withdraws
Even as you stand and stare?

And as the lifting up of sky in spring
Enlarges men within and they grow taller
Eyeing it, so we before this thing
We could not enter, no, nor even the painter
Who brain beheld, whose brushstrokes hold it forever
Could enter there.

The Elegists

Arches and towers
Of green or gold or crimson
Banner October,
And the leaves
Tumble.

What can I utter
Of all this pomp and splendour
Somber and mortal
No bird has
Sung of?

Mourned for? I shall go
Harken to every sparrow's
Elegy before
The first flake
Circle.

The Word of Water

The word of water spoke a wavy line
To the Egyptians; we can also hear
Variations from the strict linear
In fall and faucet, pail and ice-pitcher.
Whether in fountain or in porcelain
It speaks a speech so crystal in its chime
We never think to question this cold
Transparent wanderer from the underworld
About the dead,—whose resurrection fills
More than half the earth uttering a word
That no man living has interpreted.

The Last

That among all these angels
Not all angels were
Had never struck me in eternity

If a fly, a common housefly
Had not lighted on my finger.
Then a dark conjecture

Whispered some smell of earth had made it hover
Over me, whose birthplace was the fen
Where angels once had known the daughters of men.

But as I waited for some further sign
Of featherless shoulderblades and hot weather,
The fly fell dead of course,

And I returned to my arpeggios
In ceaseless Paradise
Mourning the last of flies.

To My Son

November 27, 1959

Sixteen years
Aren't very many,
Yet enough to wonder
At the world's disorder.
There is nothing older
Or newer, either,
Than mass murder.
So go on, dear son,
Ride your bicycle
Over the bleached bones
Of Political Necessity's
Last Hungary. Pedal
Under trees so tall
They are incredible
To all but you and me.
In their shade, maybe,
Though late editions cry,
And the world smoulder,
Like Beauty and like Love,
Necessity
May alter in the eye of the beholder.

Icarus

Beating his homemade wings against the sun,
Icarus was clumsy, but wing-torn
And plummeting toward the sea,
Though followed leisurely
By hosts of sunny feathers drifting down,
He found the fair arc of proportion
Which is perpetual and cannot drown.

The Factory

The thing that cannot be spoken,
And you who involved me in it,
And she too—she whose person
Burns like a banner of fire
So that I cannot shun it,

And the boy with the bad face,
He with the fish-blue eye and the tow hair
Whom I met in the alley later, wholly lost,
Answering, with malice in his answer:
"That way if you can, sir, can, sir, can, sir";

And you with the briefcase, who involved me in it,
There by the water cooler, neat as ever
When I came back in rags, burning with fever,
Smiling so reassuringly your: "Never
Shall I believe for a moment you will not win it";

And the knowing that she who burns like a banner of fire
And the boy with the bad face and the glittering leer,
And the courteous gentleman with the briefcase
Are but disguises that I chose to wear
To warn and dissuade myself from coming here.

For I failed completely, for all my mastery of time;
Discovered I should not listen, though not why;
And now as first light milks the Eastern sky
I quit the blacktop, stop the car, and see
Looming in this ploughed field, the Factory

That made me. I have found it. Overhead,
Million windows blue with sunrise.
Smelling the earth, I tread
Afraid of furrows onward to the wall
Stiller than a hospital.

On Growing Invisible

From the bland, snow-crusted eminence
Of sixty I speak to you remarking only
That if one has always wanted to be invisible
Sixty's a good place to be. Here one puts on,
Without the least strain, an impersonation
Of somebody who is only in a manner of speaking
There—hence, an excellent location
For looking far more deeply into, through
Men, women, boys, girls for traces
Of *ens* in their fixed faces,
While their patrolling and transparent eyes
Pass over the impenetrable disguise
Of a mild smiling Cheshire gentleman
Cat of sixty fading softly away.
So my first taste of growing invisible
Is full of growing light, and yet I fear
That when such marginal opacity
As in me is dissolves to earth and air,
My vision will continue to expand
Brobdingnagian
Until I comprehend all humankind
Without being there.

Being Known

Simply through being known
All ugliness is forgiven,
Whether a popular song
Or a piece of pottery.
A lopsided vase or a tune
Encountered over again
In a country or time
Sinister and withdrawn
Makes recognition
Shine in everything,
Shine and overshine
Hamlet and house and tree.
Ugly or beautiful,
It was a part of me
Exiled, denied, foregone,
We say, who cannot be
Happy till all come home.

The Party Overhead

Agonist, knocker on water pipes
Because I throw this party overhead,
Yes, it is very late as you have said,
Night thickens—but my party swells and ripes
Faster than hand can cut and bind, fits tighter
Than barns are built for. It is very great.
Still you beat time like a bad typewriter
Pounding the pipes that bring you water, sweat
Because my guests make merry, and forget
That over all that you must settle for
I send you also peace. It will not do
The slightest good to speak to the manager.
I am the manager. Your place is set.
The party overhead is thrown for you.

The Story of Jim and Hannah

Scouring the town for any opening
At all, with business tighter everywhere,
Jim saw Hannah rocking in a chair
On the hotel porch, embroidering
Something he couldn't see in a round frame.
When their eyes met, acceleration
Took over. They were pledged within the same
Day, married in a week; throughout the nation
Business blossomed like a sunflower
As if to make them prosper. Hannah shone
Bright in his heart and brain—but every hour
Shrank to a minute, year to a day. "Slow down,"
His doctor said, "You can afford it, Jim."
Then he stopped dead. Hannah embroidered him.

For All the People Who Are Waiting

Even now, he realized, he could still turn back:
The shriek of the chainsaw he had heard in bed
Did not augur well for the day ahead;
And buildings going up and coming down,
The ceaseless thud of riveters all over town
Left small time for the contemplation
Of veritable ends. He shunned the blat
Of media against all faces set
Beyond the City of Destruction.
He took no stock in it because he knew
How many jubilant at setting out
Now squatted in some tin-tarpaper shack
Between the gasworks and the railroad track
Waiting for time's slow mellowing. Always now
He saw their faces, yellow, white, and black,
Grow angrier and thinner as more and more
Age altered everything except their lack
Till just the going on, the not waiting
Any more was all they dreamed, the only
Living thing, until—quite suddenly—
They were not living. Lines must be cut, torn down,
Communication blocked, lest blue men
Lock them in Destruction, that great city.
Should they do that he'd cut throats gladly,
He thought, then thought again:
When throats are cut there's no more talking then.

Sonnet

It is the grinding that we fear the most,
The kneading of the heart against the bone—
The first, being partly fire and partly ghost,
Hammers unreconciled the living stone
Until it break, collapsing on the host
Whose inn became a cell, himself the toast
He had to mutter now the guests were gone.
Yet sometimes he will fill his lungs with air
And contemplate the large, blue, open sky;
And seeing all the room there is up there
More fiercely beat the wall, more loudly cry,
And while the bone withstands him never ceases
Until this grinding shatters both to pieces.

Mouth-Honor, Breath

For Arnold Kenseth

Being is all, and to have been there
Better by far than never to have gone;
But heat, cold, wet, dry, hunger, and storm
Make being and footing antithetical,
And mouth-honor, breath is, after all, warm.

The Ministry of Communication
Gets few requests for clarification
These days—so many clerks have gone
Who told the truth in legible signs—the walls
Of all the stalls attest
Who shall be king hereafter; with one voice
Salute Macbeth.

Memorandum for Yalta

The law and prophets hang
On changing human nature. This is not done
By pack or memorandum. It is done
By bringing Caliban
Loaded with chains to Prospero, who now
Lives in obscure retirement in Milan.

Spring Poem

It works on words, itself invisible, holds
Flattery in defiance, mastering
Syllable by syllable, again
And yet again, the lineaments of man.

And when the sunset gun
Bids blind day be quiet, and the mole
Peers out in sightless curiosity,
Bewildered, happy, certain it is free,
Not knowing what it's free for, but aware

What the wind feels like, poetry is there
Eyeing the world in its reality
Condemning still
Botched passion, mortgaged will,
Affirming by the act of being there
Man, who walks among the stones of fire
Yet a little while.

Oakleaf Elegy

Oakleaves clinging to the bough,
God knows how,
Spring's sinister spectators, skinny now,
Make music paper-thin
Until the March wind whistles and they go
Head over tail down to
The town of no more dancing, where no light
Falls on dome or avenue or height
And music soft and subterranean
Laps them till they become
A part and portion of the lower town
And cannot recollect the upper one.

To the Young Rebels

What the heart wants comes true.
Therefore be sure you
Do what you want. Look how many
Condescend to war's felicity. Stare

Where you will, you will discover no
Alternative hid from the trilobite;
History is adamant: you
Are what *it* willed to do.

Oh wonderful consensus! *Schrechlichkeit*
Falls from the air. Certainly
Men of low degree are vanity
And men of high a lie. So now
When all men know
That Gabriel has a horn
Able to blow
Rebellion and the Establishment alike
To the ionosphere, now, if you know
What you want, do, do, do, do, do.

The Stones of Sleep

The Germans rub it on
The walls of their houses.
The gray, transparent stone
Assures the inhabitant
No matter what he does, what he has done
A sleep so plaisant and so wholesome
As he may never wholly waken from.

The Onion, the Lacewing, and the Mole

The onion, the lacewing, and the mole
  Once set in motion
Burgeon, on the whole — till they put on
  Nothing at all —

Quite predictably. In our kind
  The pattern's less defined
And yet a sort of luminous cartoon
  Hovers in Hölderlin,

Dante and Blake, but only to disclose
  Ecstatic imprecision:
The central radiance of the mystic Rose
  Out-dazzles vision

Lest we should perceive futurity
  Unrolled before our own
Eyes and forfeit liberty along
  With lacewing, mole, onion.

Note on Modern Journalism During the Last Campaign

Butter and ink
Butter and ink
When we have enough butter
We print what we think,

But ink without butter
Ink without butter
And we publish whatever
You want us to utter.

Of Angels

Your angel weighs heavier than your mortal.
It hurts like hell if you run into one.
Only one wrestler ever made an angel cry uncle.

When they leap off the world it is as though
Washington Monument flew,
The whole world wobbles like a soap-bubble. Hang on!
One will be leaving any minute now.

Hymn to Time

In the vast shadow I was still alive
To the going on of things, of butterflies
Tenderly examining weeds, the flourishing
Leaves of peppermint, black-eyed susans, daisies.
There seemed to be no steadiness or stasis
Such as Joyce saw in the going on of things.
So I began to set down stealthy praises
Of such as these, rocks too, of course, and trees
Of all sorts, especially elms, and grasses
And summer clouds transacting leisurely masses;
And porpoises, and all fish in all seas
And goldfish bowls shared my indifferent praises.
Nor was I unaware
Of the tribes and nations of the air
Gathering for colloquy and prayer
When the cone of shadow comes down
With the first dew.
Not in me dwelt, I knew,
Ability to renew
Movement in any flesh and bone drawn
By the horizon.

Envoi

Running out of town on a rail is too good for
The little king and his sister
They say who yesterday
(The good days seem so far!)
We threw up our hats, shouted ourselves hoarse for.

"Wisdom will die with you . . . vox populi"
The preacher says, and no doubt it's true, though
If this wheel keeps turning over and over,
Who'll put a spoke in it or brake the day
When they are suddenly we, we suddenly they?

Goodbye then, little princess and little king,
For awhile. We cannot honestly entertain
Hope for you now, but neither can we deny
That somewhere an ear already hears the barrow
Rumbling on stone that will run us out tomorrow.

The Doomed City

The doomed city we live in
Is crumbling while we sit
Discussing it.

The clock upon the height
Moves interminably from left to right
But we are not
Interminable. "I'm

Very gloomy about things
But you have to make yourself
Keep trying anyway,"
Said Bobby Kennedy

Knowing eternity
Does not open to the bodily eye.
We must look far
Inward to perceive
Here in the doomed city where we live
The city that will not die.

A Goodnight

The wood dark
The dark great
The hour late
And none to mark;

Underhill,
Curled in a ball,
One lies still
In bolt hole;

Yet lifts ear
Now and again.
Fear you not,
Small one.

Your pursuit
Slumbers deep
Under the earth.
You too sleep,

Till the sun
Sniffs through the dew
After you,
Then wake. Then run.

On the Night Train from Oxford

Once we were small and real
Who in this freezing shell
Whisk through the dark. The guard
Who slammed the door of our cell

Shut sight from our eyes;
So swiftly turn the wheels
We cannot feel what we know,
We cannot know what we feel.

A number of years ago
Hulme took the classic view:
Man is limited,
He said, but the world said *No*.

Man is boundless and good
And will make all things new
Look out the window, Look
At what we have done and do.

By this compartment flit
The fragments of an age.
Who can put back together
Our bombed-out heritage?

Today at New College
Epstein's *Lazarus*
Heard one call his name,
Rose, towered over us,

Loomed in his cerement,
Twisting his narrow head
Back and *Up* to the Word
Compelling him from the dead.

Surely Epstein knew
It could speak to anyone,
Gentile or Jew, even
To one on this night train.

Speak Distortion
Back to the Human Form
Through light that seems pure pain
Back to the living sun.

The Shift

I stood in a room I knew, a beautiful room
Where on bright rugs and furniture a-gleam
The sun shone, but now it was time to go.
I passed the door and entered the dark hall
But half way down turned and peered back and knew
That what I saw was not the room at all
But a flat picture seen as under glass.
I shrugged and sauntered on. What good does it do
To caterwaul? This alteration
Is instantaneous and will go on
Till memory is the only thing in the world.

Variations

I

The richness of alone is like down,
Swansdown, yet it rings.
Voices without sound
Say things
Say things.

II

Auden's cool commentary
Instructed us
In where we were; he knew
Where we were heading, too,
But chose to refrain
From telling us too distinctly
Knowing
He would be elsewhere
When the crunch came.

Elegy

Terror and knowledge, criticism and
The mutilation of philosophy—
Spring thunder mingling with the guns—
Converge and we are here. How many hands
Furious, laborious, patient
Plucked, pulled, nudged, pointed, crushed and beckoned us
To this gray street corner
At this dividing hour?

No doubt, no doubt at all,
Wedged against the wall,
What thunderous cortege and funeral
Passes the city square.
Now pace the paired black horses trapped in jet
Now mourners in black coaches hung with crepe
Bury hope, bury the world's hope. Slowly
The wheels turn, slowly it starts to rain.

Who killed it, then? Who in a mailcoach once
Went whipping under sheets of moonlight
Spreading the tidings of world victory,
And as the horses reeled a wooded curve
Galloping thunder to the steady stars,
Who saw the light barouche, one wavering there?
And did he grasp the coachman's arm? Point? Yell?
Or sit, to speak or move incapable?

Bury the world's hope with lamentation
And as it sinks to cold clay bow your head
And whisper as you do
I saw and knew and could not lift my hand.
Yet as you go still carry in your mind
The precious lens Spinoza, the Dutch Jew
Ground to a diamond's water:
Peace is not absence of war

But the virtue born of the vigor of the soul.
He knew Man is not God nor God Nature
Yet in this man persisted still the vigor
To seek the good and do it, and his word
To us is that of Christian at the River:
I leave my sword
To him who follows after me, my skill
To him who can get it.

Journey's End

Thus hope subsided little by little
—Robert Lowell

Little by little, friend,
Hope and joy end.
There is no room for them
In Jerusalem
But only for the true.
I cannot think that you
Can care about such vanity
While you suffer sanity.
And what is that? Why just
What you feel. Gray dust
Falls on everything else,
And the true were false
If I see your face
Other than it is
As pure, as clear, as strange.
Nothing can alter change.
Moving from star to star
What we really are
Is lonely. Lovers blend
Only at journey's end.

Karl was right

To make a poem
You just grab hold of a word
Sticking out of your mind
And keep pulling. This
Is a queer one, though,
Greyish green and
Doubled on itself,
Seems to be coming out
In a knotted loop
It's nothing but a snarl
Soft as velvet, a round
Greyish green hullabaloo
With a hole in the middle.
And now
There's nothing I can do
About that hole but watch it widen
While I and all my colleagues stand
Clad in our best academic regalia
Hand in hand
But stepping back a bit from time to time
(Come in there more of you)
Watching it widen.
Can we surround, contain
It?
Are there enough of us
To mask this ever widening abyss
Containing only space and the dank water
That leaks down from the fractured sewer pipes?

The Coral

Every human dream
Abandoned and let fall
Under the sea-swell
As polyp hardens on.

Hence many a sturdy hull
Has foundered in blue calm.
The dreamed but never done
Binds the sea with cruel coral.

The Death of The Poor

(after Baudelaire)

Only Doctor Death can make us well,
The cure of living is our only hope,
Our flagon where we pluck up heart to quell
Winter and night upon the darkest slope.
Through snow that falls forever, ever fell
We see the lantern-glimmer from the door
Of an old famous tavern where they sell
Victual and ease for bones all travel sore.
He lifts us up and leads us by the hand
By gentle passages to Samarkand
And smoothes the golden bed where we shall lie.
He is the only thing we understand,
Our bread, our treasure, our own native land,
Our gate swung open in the alien sky.

When the Long Day

When the long day turns
And the lights in the street come on
But daylight lingers it is betweentimes
When everything that is
Might have been different. Eyes
Gently enfranchised see
Nothing that is or was has ever been
Entirely itself, perfect and whole.
So in the turning of the long day
Between the streetlights and the failing sun
Glimmers again
The City we left, the City we long for
Betweentimes but cannot enter now.

Walking Eastward

I'm walking eastward at five when everyone
Else let loose from office, shop, and clock,
Lock and lock-step and honking every horn
Homes in the level sun.

I don't know how or when
Everything turned around.
It was not so last year.
Time vanished—better so—
As it was lived. To know
What lay around the bend
My only care. But now
Like salmon up rock torn
Rapids, I leap, I spin
Eastward toward my home
Love, end, and origin.

House

House
Vast and ambiguous
Which was before we were

Did you
Build yourself and then grow populous
By taking thought, or

Did someone leave a tap on long ago
In you
Which with its spatter

Affirms at the very least a householder
Who will return at last if only to
Turn off the water.

Song A La Mode

Now let us sing a song in praise
Of atonality.
Poets have been phasing out the pear-shaped tones
In deference—it could be—
To Richard Strauss, Schoenberg, Debussy.
And now in the magnificent uproar
Of clashing consonants, you're
Lucky if you hear a true rhyme
Even at Easter or at Christmas time.

No Orpheus

Men rise up and sink back into the black.
How can you tell the dead from the living? The clack
Of footheels in the midnight parking lot
May just be some attendant who has not
Quit for the night and for some ungodly reason
Is still hanging around. It may be the season
(Pre-spring), or the time of night (12:03 o'clock),
But the whole situation is enough to block
My going home the ordinary way.
I take an alley never seen by day
Into another empty as the moon
Of living man. Here there is no one,
For the dead are only people who lived "then,"
Not "now," and I'm "now," but again
It could be that I've taken the wrong fork
In time as space. May they not interlock
These "nows"? No light from any window here
Speaks of the living, and now sharp and clear
Heel-taps. What do I lead? If I look round
Will it melt back silent underground?
I hurry, and the footsteps ring behind
There are lights ahead. I shall not change my mind.
Whether or not time loops upon its track,
I am no Orpheus, will not look back.

A Fair Warning

Practically everyone goes to the Petrified Forest
As visitor or tourist,
Staying no longer than permits of the barest
"We drove through Saturday. Every contortion
Of those grim trunks staggers imagination."

But once in a great while among these strong
Motionless boughs and leaves unwhispering
One stands as if he heard
A petrified bird
And stays long.

Serpent

The serpent said: Forgive me, being serpent,
I always have possessed the power of speech
But since the Fall have grown more taciturn
And seldom bother with words except as now
For critical instruction. Did you know
That Kingston, New Jersey was the capital
Of the United States for several months
During General Washington's last campaign?
And may be so again if what goes on in Washington
Goes on. But I'm not here
To talk politics. I mean, damn it,
Look about you. What do you think
Of this lovely tree with all the apples on it?

At The Louvre

After so many larger canvases
I thought with surprise at first *How small she is*
Next I grew aware she was looking at me
Smiling a little like a good hostess
To put me at my ease, but also
To know me through and through. Leonardo
Had her eyes; they are hers now
To study all who pass until the lens
Blur or the world runs out of specimens.

The Let Go

Let go out of the mill into the meadow,
We find our hands fall. Nothing will do
We thought might sweetly pass the time
Except rock, trees, unchanging hills, enormous
Cumuli voyaging around the world
With all deliberate speed;—these and the animals
Our only study and our studio.
If Plato did not lie and the world indeed
Have a living soul, only the let go
May look upon it wondering and know.

The Way

This is the way
It must be
Not just for you, me,
But everyone. Put
Your right foot down, and then,
Just under it, is something
Molding itself to meet it.
So everyone who dares
Can walk in this cold air
Steadily
Though no one be in sight—
May never be. Only be sure
One foot goes out and
Down, and, so far,
Something under lifts to meet it. So
Ridiculously
We make our way on what we cannot know.

Why People Avoid Poetry

Our Lord's "Lead us not into temptation"
Is more correctly translated, scholars say—
Uncomfortably but less preposterously—
"Put us not to the test." Oh misery,
We cry, make us not see
Ourselves in any poem's transparency.
Deliver us, dear Lord, from ever knowing
Who we really are, what we are doing.

The Soul

"The soul is—well—the soul," said Browning's Prior
To the young Lippi. Fifteen hundred years
Of intricate theology, and now
All he could offer was tautology.
Yet he was right. And in the shifting sands
Of this our Dead Sea shore the soul appears
And loves, unreasonably, on and on.

Loves like Narcissus? Loves itself, then?
No, for it has none (myth and mud-picture,
Bloody, pathetic, hugged and horrid doll,
Sheet left fluttering in the horny hands
Of the disciple when the young man ran
Naked away, inapprehensible
Alike by Peter and the constable.)

Loves because it was made of nothing and flung
Naked to this hot sun.
And, though this earth from Cancer to the Pole
Were pitiless sunlight on unarable soil,
Would see each creature from sand-flea to man
As diamond, irreplaceable diamond. The soul
Loves all, for love makes no comparison.

The Searchers

The argument of wonder is the end
Of all our striving. Half a loaf sustains
Nobody long, and all our joys blend
In their long race with pain

To pierce the unintelligible where
Sight is not, nor sound, and the last sense
Stumbling upon its own incognizance
Waits for a flash from some nerve-ending: here

Is our country. Only, we who once made
Trifles of terrors, moving unafraid
Over those dreadful vortices now feel
The argument of wonder at our keel,

And balancing our corporal bones upon
A winged equation steer
Past starlight's last diminishing and lone
Pinpoint of knowledge toward an unknown fear.

Failure

Failure is more important than success
Because it brings intelligence to light
The bony structure of the universe.

The Song They Sang

First Voice

Hurry, piercing gray water unwounded, fly
Straight as a homing missile or flung stone.
We shall receive you gently, mariner.
All you desire shall be done.

Second Voice

Hurry, the waves around will never grow
Less plaintive, trammelled, gray.
The silver service is laid out on the table,
Dinner is served, why is the guest away?

Third Voice

On this ship where no one knows you,
Nor knows he is alone, be alone and know,
Helpless with déjà vu, watching the strange
Obliging, outlying islands file by.

All

The neutral forts and fieldworks, neutral sky
Greet you (though fire and pain
Nuzzle the tender skulls of all things born
Elsewhere). This is the money comb

You gnaw in dreams and wake to hunger's pang,
The skyline of bright gold. Far-wanderer
Behold your consummation.
                          Thus they sang.
The sailors, bending to their oars, rowed on.

Conrad Aiken, Goodbye

Conrad Aiken, goodbye,
You whose gray-blue eye
So many ghosts had seen
That we, Francis and I,
Seeing you, saw one
Stocky, blond, young
Yet translucent, of another plane;
Aiken who lunched with two
Bugeyed students at the Georgian
Back in the twenties. (That spring
You had been tutoring
At Harvard. *Blue*
Voyage had just appeared.) "For me," you said,
"The worst moment of voyage is setting out,
The rising up and sinking down but not
Moving on, the scent of bilge pervasive,
The crate-and-garbage-strewn
Dock and dock-water. I always swallow
Mothersills then. It helps me over
The interface and queasy of reprise.
Once out of harbor on the high seas
A dynamism, whether of voyage or verse
Operates. You see through veil on veil
Of mist or fog the new psychology
Until all vanishes." You said, and vanished.
Aiken, it was in pure
Generosity you let us see you
Near as across the table, at the end
Of one voyage, the beginning of another
Cosmic great traverse that still goes on
Peeling the universal, the soul's onion
To Nothing or Eternity. Goodbyes
Many
Many
Many
Go out to you from this

Ship of earth we ride and you despised
All but its rich cargo of images,
And may the Mothersills of human praise
Comfort your setting out. Good voyage! Good voyage!

In This Warm and Silent Cube

for William Reese

In this warm and silent cube
With the winds of winter roaring
Over the roof, under the flooring,
I, who by good luck am smoking
Tubes of tobacco and exploring
Mind's supreme initial, find
Matter hardly to my mind:
Namely, Thomas Hobbes's cool
Refutation of the soul:
"Material immaterial."

Yet the figure has its pith:
Contradiction fathers myth.
And your oxymoron, Tom,
Past the toadstool of the Bomb,
And the politics of Man,
The death-sweat of Leviathan,
All the terror you foresaw
Shall creep, shall rise, shall be made whole.
All passes save the metaphor
And oxymoron of the soul.

This Wind

This is the wind that blows
Everything
Through and through.

I wouldn't toss a kitten
Knowingly into a wind like this,
But there's no taking

Anything living
Out of the fury
Of this wind we breathe and ride upon.

We Still Must Follow

We still must follow through brush and through briar
The mystery of things but never say
Supernatural, a useless term
Omitted from our proper dictionary
Because it mocks all definition.
Everything, everything can be explained
Once *modus operandi* is laid bare
And pixies, kobolds, gnomes, and elves probably
Have nothing to do with the case. Admittedly,
We still have a long way to go to explain
Everything, but we've made a good start,
And damned be he who first cries "miracle."

Stone

Look at a stone and it's nothing,
Something to kick against, but look at the
Same stone twenty years later
And you feel yourself vanishing in perspective into thin air.

There have always been sacred stones
And this must be one reason: stone's soul
Came to its confirmation, conformation
So ploddingly

It clings to one idea
While we go on to others smaller, smoother
Than the granite boulder
That struck the armed guard from the tomb door
And set the prisoner free,

Stupor mundi, amazement of beholders.
Thank you, stone
For being of the same opinion still
For being Peter, whom
We shall deny, return to, differ from
Until the sky is rolled up like a scroll
And all the stars fall down.

From Manuscript

Stone

(Variant)

Look at a stone and it's nothing,
Something to kick against, but look at the
Same stone twenty years later
And you feel yourself vanishing in perspective into thin air.

There have always been sacred stones and this must be one reason:
Stone's soul
Moved toward its conformation, confirmation
So ploddingly
It clings to one idea
While we go on to others smaller, smoother
Than the granite boulder's
That struck aside the guard at the sealed door
And set the prisoner free,
Stupor mundi.
                    The amazement of beholders
Cannot last long, nor can this Indian Summer
And halcyon day of ours
With all its autumn flowers,
Its maple and its sumac. Thank you, stone,
In the world's defoliation and its fall
And in its winter chill
For being of the same opinion still.

Inquit Natura

These
Are not what they are,
Unlike trees.

Because they raise
Micturate mountains of effluvia
Floods cannot wash away in forty days,

Except by hearsay and by say-so,
It does not follow
They ever were or ever will be

Human. I only see
Stalling amphibia
Half in, half out of water.

I cannot wait much longer.
Hear, Bottleneck,
The whole universe honking at your back!

When All Our Hours Touch Hands

When all our hours touch hands
And with a golden glance
Pierce us also with the shining thread
That binds all creatures, lest they fall apart
Lifeless and aloof, that shine so clear,
In joy and fear

We look right through the mask of rime and snow
And in this living sun
See all our mortal hours converge in one
Irresistible paean
That we our true love know
From stock and stone.

And every world is strung,
And Time, on such a beam
(Flesh cannot bear it long),
From here to the last gleam,
Their single song thanksgiving
For being given, to the Giver of being.

Salt

Foam flung off the sea
seasons with salt the stone.
Salt as the waves they prowl
Are petrel, tern and gull.

Carthage was salted down
By imperial Rome.
All victory is salt,
Not honey in the comb.

Once When I Was Five on a Rainy Day

Once when I was five on a rainy day
Grandma taught me a new game (there's no
Boredom like a five year old's kept in).
She found a glass bowl with a crinkly rim
And two spools, one with black thread on it, the other bare.
She dropped the black one in the bowl and told me
"Now wind the thread on the empty spool." I did
And it was sort of fun. The spinning spool
Tinkled musically till the thread was gone
And if it still rained I'd swap and start again
So on a rainy autumn afternoon
The full grew empty and the empty full
And I learned about History, how it goes round
And around, Spring, Summer, Autumn, Winter,
And then around again, but what God does
On good days when
There's no need to stay in out of the rain
Grandma didn't explain.

Fugitive

(Variant of A Goodnight)

The wood dark,
The dark great,
The hour late
And none to mark,

Lie still
Curled in a ball
In your bolt-hole
Under the hill,

Yet prick your ears
Now and again
For the breath and the foot
Of the pursuit,

But that also
Must sleep and rest;
You sleep, too,
Until the East

Lets slip the sun
To sniff your prints
Where you have gone.
Then wake, and run.

Sorry, Saint Augustine

Bright, indignant eye
Blazing across fourteen centuries:
Call not that the final good
Which ends goodness,

Well, if I may make myself a tongue
For my fellow citizens, I guess
You don't need to worry, Augustine:
We serve THE BRAIN, and THE BRAIN'S will is this:

To seek the Enemy
In every alley, pothole, gully, crater
And puff him into vapor.
In his name we labor

To pluck out of ourselves to the last fiber
Passion, compunction, breathing blood and bones;
In his memory banks is our peace;
Decision his alone.

We serve our ends as Jerome served Jerome's,
Perfectly, till flesh no more intrude
Or crawl about the Cybernetic City,
The BRAIN'S beatitude.

A Further View

There is no giggling in this classroom,
Whispering, shuffling of books and papers, I'm
Alone at my desk in front of empty chairs
Where I have been for almost thirty years,
Though there were times I thought a class attended.
Now, thinking back, I know better, having amended
The earlier, more charitable view:
I know it was myself I talked to.
Now this is very strange, for my discourse
Is salted with little jokes (quite mild, of course,)
And simple illustrations (all concrete)
As though a wafted snore from a back seat
Had warned me people here with grades to get
Must stay awake for twenty minutes yet.
And so I have arrived by fits and starts
At a philosophy of style — of sorts.
It adds to this: But never, never
Say simply what you really feel; be clever:
Use indirection and make crystal clear
What you don't mean to people who aren't there.

Untitled

All trees at evening murmur—
So far down have words come
From the high place where language rich with sun
Shines in its own translucency, but our
Syllables fall from our lips like stone.

Untitled

Only be sure of this:
Nothing recedes like success; Beauty itself
Flashes past, grass withers, flowers fade,
But Beauty is the promise of happiness
Even as Nietzsche said. Though every glade
And every hill where human foot has stepped
Glisters with glass of broken promises,
Be of good cheer: this promise will be kept.

Knowing

Perfect love, says John,
Casts out fear, but a demon
Roosting on my shoulder says, *If so,*
Perfect knowledge casts out hope. Muskrat,
Rabbit and you alike fall short of that
Which we who dwell within the Tree of Light
Foreknow, and knowing are not fortunate.

Senex et Infans

Dancing! said the old man in the wheelchair,
There's nothing like it. In Aldebaran
It whirls around forever
Beyond fatigue and hunger,
And even in Altair
Everyone dances. They dance everywhere
But here. Let go, nurse-man,
Let me go dancing in my old wheelchair!

The Magnificent

From the New Hospital your eye looks down
Over worn, gray three-deckers to the brown
Sluiceway or canal under the hill
That powers our cotton mill.

And almost every day,
If you look at the right time, in the right way,
You see eight sea-gulls on the water-wall.
Strong, white-breasted, sabre-beaked, and tall
They dive, poise, and return
In just parabola
As in a dance figure.

With mutual deference and courtesy,
They take their aliment,
And though the waters of the sluiceway
Bear dye, excerpted tonsils, excrement,
Each taken morsel turns a living thing
Wholly magnificent,
Descending and returning with beak full,
At the foot of the hill, near the new hospital.

The Two Orders

Poetry like death imposes
Order on the hands and face
That in life were various.
Taken up into this place
Where injustice is forgiven
Every girl a poet has praised
Enters Beatrice and is lost
In transcendence, while the human
Eye perceives the living woman.

Beauty, truth, and charity,
Joy and all simplicity
In disorder do not lie.
Where these gentle sisters ply
Thread and needle
Set the table
Dust the dust
Rock the cradle,
(Though the furniture be hay
And the living room a stable)
Nothing is disorderly.

But the order of the dead
Is composed of silences
Ranged behind the moving word,
Smell of grass and taste of bread
Rank on rank they wheel away
Past astronomy where they
Witness what is wholly true
Or death were disorder too.

Hit Or Myth?

You will see me running through the air
Sweating like Moses, and perchance will say,
"Comforter, what comfort is out there?"
But I shall answer nothing, being then
Merely allegorical, a figure
Drawn out of time for your instruction.
And you will run your fingers through your hair
And turn away, certain this allegory
Does not apply to you, but look down,
See how your legs like pistons wakening
Run faster, faster, faster, God knows where.

For Prisoners

After a little while
The bars of bone
That hold you
Will wear thin. The waters wear
The stones, the winds bear
The dust of stones elsewhere.
Soon, prisoner,
You who once were free
As a breath of air will be
With earth and sea and sky
In one autonomy.

Closer

Closer to the bone
And closer to the bottom of the bag
But also closer
To the land where the Jumblies live,
Farther and fewer all the time—
Yet still the job remains
Of naming with names things that pass.
Of things that pass, this is the maker's task,
Lest Time's red herring
Fool the running hound
Of essence, or confound
The scent of eternity with Time's dry bromage.

A Song for Sanctuaries

Sun in my eyes, traffic into the sun
Dustily glittering, and all these
Sparrows. They drown our honking with their peeping,
And in the rush-hour's setting,
Whirling, gossiping, fighting, defecating,
Blur tall buildings. If the drift toward war
Plunges to Armageddon, let there be
Somewhere some towers like these left standing
Windowless as fortress and repose
For these quick citizens. When overthrown
By ticker-tape, strangled by telephone,
The son of man lies still, let them go on.
And let the population of the sparrows
Thicken at evening as the sun goes down.

Close To Us

Close to us, yet higher up than all
The blue sky arches downward in the sun
Toward the horizon. Since all seeing is
A kind of touching, we can feel it fall
To the world's edge and rest on houses there.
So human townships touch eternity
And may be painted in one picture so.
And so with us, whether we tread the earth
Or ride the air, these two confront each other
But never speak their names, written in water
And in the shadow of clouds, and you, and me.

The Twins

Everybody is the thing also
That he is coming to.
Having stubbed your toe or cut your finger,
It shocks you when you find
Such familiar matters on your mind,

Yet educates: pain strides
Undiscovered continents; and tides
No ship has yet divided pain shall claim,
Lifting the flag of consciousness like flame
In the king's name.

When pain drives in its bitter wedge between
Your valiance and your dust,
Each sees the other as it might have been,
And though it seems not just
Your thinghood and your ghost
Should be divided for a little while—
A heartbeat or an aeon—one must go
To cast no shadow, one to fill a hole;
Yet one from one shall still be one: you, you,
When the great wheel comes full.